Retailing in Colours

Dear Christine,

Enjoy o.

All the best!o

Doug

Retailing in Colours

Your Guide to Better Understanding
YOUR Customers "How to be
of Exceptional Service"

Guy L Moisan & Doug Atkinson

ISBN: 1515160459
ISBN 13: 9781515160458

ABOUT THE AUTHORS

Guy L. Moisan has been working in the field of Human Resources for over 30 years, from Eastern to Western Canada including the far North of Nunavik. He has also been working with True Colors International for approximately 20 years as a Facilitator and Master Trainer. True Colors, a personality profiling tool, is an easy and entertaining way to identify your own character spectrum to better understand yourself and others.

Guy first discovered True Colors in 1993 when attending a 'True Colors' workshop. The program was simple, applicable in all aspects of life and provided a positive understanding of 'Self'. 'True Colors' was the motivation required to bring to the surface the tools he is so passionate to share with you today.

Guy has had the great privilege of hosting seminars across Canada, the United States and Japan. In doing so, he has touched and worked with a wide variety of organizations, from large retail corporations to non-profit organizations and from education to the military (both the Canadian and US military).

Guy enjoys working in the world of "What can I do". A global leader within the world of colour profiling, he also motivates, creates and has no limitation to what he or anyone around him can do. His passion is for the development of self-awareness.

Read, let the fun begin ☺

Doug Atkinson is pleased to join the Leading with Colours team. With 28 years of training and coaching experience in Canada and the United States, Doug has trained and entertained thousands of retail professionals to become better and more efficient sellers using product knowledge, humour and an increased understanding of people at all levels.

Doug is a sought after speaker at many trade shows and has been featured on numerous news programs, magazines, television and radio programs. Through his training, Doug has helped hundreds of salespeople achieve their goals both for themselves and for their clients. He has received the most important awards that are available in Canada both for training and service to the community. Doug Atkinson is the recipient of the Cosmetic Outstanding Service Award (COSA) for Training 2005 and has also received the Canadian Cosmetics Careers Association Award of Merit in 2006. He is also honored to be a member of the Cosmetic Techniques and Management Program Advisory Committee at Seneca College in Toronto.

Doug has personally worked one-on-one with thousands of individuals to help make their goals a reality. Bringing a constant evolving perspective to learning that centers on engagement and enthusiasm as catalyst for change.

Dedications to

From Guy; To Laura, who has always been my support, my friend, my pillar of love, hope, and mostly my encouragement throughout this whole process.

From Doug; I would like to dedicate this book to my partner Gary who has been the one to encourage me to strive to a new level and who has never let me down.

I would also like to thank my sisters, Marcia, Paula and Carol who have been there for me all my days.

ACKNOWLEDGEMENTS TO

Our friends Mark Cahill, Katrina White, Danette Fento-Menzie, Grahame Gerstenberg and Pablo Etchegaray Albanell for their continuous support in the development of this book.

TABLE OF CONTENTS

INTRODUCTION

Retail has been defined as: "the process of selling consumer goods and/or services to customers through multiple channels of distribution to earn a profit. Demand is created through diverse target markets and promotional tactics, satisfying consumers' wants and needs through a lean supply chain." Websters dictionary

As store owners, entrepreneurs, sales representatives or CEO's of organizations, your task is to ensure that the sales of goods or commodities in small or large quantities be done directly to consumers. To create a relationship 'Whether it be personal or virtual' with your customers, so that each and every one of your customers are prepared to promote your products and/or services.

Your goal is to help your customers feel that you and your staff have taken exceptional care of them and fulfilled their needs.

Our goal is to share with you our years of experience, our observations and our studies in the world of retail and human behaviour. How to apply a simple too that all can enjoy and use every single day at work.

This book is specifically created for all retail organizations and services and will provide you with tools, examples and ideas to identify your customers' personality style quickly and accurately. Specifically, how to address and work with your customer according to your evaluation of their colour spectrum.

As you read, you will recall many of your own personal experiences, successes and failures when attempting to deal with a specific client. When applying your own experiences to any new learning method it creates a personal attachment to what you are learning, it makes it real.

In addition, this book will provide you with clarity as to Who you are, a simple view of '**Self**' and the answer to **"Who am I?"**

"Why This Matters"

So many of us walk through life trying to act like someone else, being told how to present ourselves in a crowd, to speak, eat, etc. Many of us don't understand why our presentation is inadequate and simply lacking compared to the person or persons we are trying to imitate, leaving us with the feeling of consistent failure. Having the ability to recognize yourself and your personal colour spectrum will assist in your personal growth within the organization. It will help you to answer the question **"How and why do I present myself this way?"**

The second benefit is recognizing others. Rather than trying to regulate the behaviour of others, we will guide you on a path of understanding others. As you learn how to identify your customer's colours, you will know how to work with customers, you will have the ability to provide them with exactly what they need and/or want. Knowing their values, and how they would like to be treated will help avoid the possibility of stressing them and creating a very unhappy shopping experience.

When you understand and value your customers, for who they truly are, they will respond to you in a fashion of utmost gratitude and will want to work with you every single time they visit, making you the '**Go to person**' and business.

The retail world has been a part of our culture for centuries, beginning with trading and bartering. Times have changed, however, some things have not. Some of our customers like to chat, some are quality and price conscience, some are always in a rush and some just cannot make up their minds due to lack of information.

'Retailing in Colours' will help you realize that there is no right or wrong way of addressing someone.

Being yourself is the natural way of dealing with customers, but also paying attention to the customers' colour style will allow you to enter their world and be part of their own personal shopping adventure.

In our experience, we have gone through many ups and downs with supervisors, staff and most importantly, customers. Let us share with you our easy and simple way to work with everyone around you and achieve incomparable results and end up with very satisfied customers.

Your customer doesn't care how much you know until they know how much you care.

Damon Richards

WHERE DO WE COME FROM?

Personality traits have been dissected for thousands of years. The common question is **"What are we all about?"** We have dated some studies as far back as 400BC: from Hippocrates (370 to 460 BC), to Carl Jung (1920's), to Myers-Briggs (MBTI) (1950's) and many others. We are not here to teach you a history lesson - it surely was not our strong point in school. Nevertheless, it is vital for us to supply you with the validity of where our information came from. Let's begin.

A very popular philosopher in the medical world, Hippocrates, is known for the creation of the Hippocratic Oath. His studies of people were of the general population, using the fluids of the body as a framework. His terms and identification tools were Sanguine, Choleric, Phlegmatic and Melancholic.

Next on our list of significant profilers is Carl Jung. Jung was a student at the University of Basel in 1895-1900, studying biology, zoology, paleontology and archaeology. Mostly interested in philosophy, mythology and early Christian literature, his curiosity in human behaviour guided him to Sigmund Freud, Jung became Freud's protégé. Jung valued the importance of distinguishing between individual psychology and psychoanalysis, which is referred to as "Analytical psychology".

His work included the development of a personality model defined as **Introversion and Extroversion.**

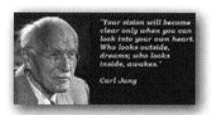

One of the most popular profile tools that is still used today, is the 'Myers/Briggs' (MBTI) Type Indicator Personality inventory. Katherine Cook Briggs and her daughter Isabel Briggs Myers wanted to find a way to help everyone understand themselves by developing a temperament model that was easier to comprehend than the challenging academic language and theories of Jung.

Consequently, MBTI was born. A system that continues to be used extensively in the world of business, education and counseling, even today.

A fourth temperament theory brings us to Kr. David Keirsey.

In the 1970's, Keirsey was a professor and department chair at California State University, in the counseling department. With the assistance of Marilyn Bates they published the book **"Please Understand Me."**

The assessment was very similar to the MBTI, but much shorter, with the intention of making this assessment a little more practical and easier to understand.

Now to our last system we will touch on, however not the only system using colours as identifiers. 'True Colors' - created by Don Lowry. In 1978 Don (*Picture of Don and his wonderful Wife Erica, our wonderful friends*) introduced the world to the True Colors concept. The start of True Colors were the live shows, made as a fun, entertaining way to acquaint people to the simple but powerful temperament typing. Participants learned of themselves in an entertaining theatrical production designed to portray extremes of the four temperament types.

Four playing cards, each of different colour, were created with illustrations specific to characteristics of each of the four temperaments and a defined colour. The cards provide a hands-on experience in discovering your own personality traits.

With respect to so many other great programs out in the world today, we have provided you with a short overview of other systems:

Leading with Colours	Blue	Green	Gold	Orange
Don Lowry's True Colors	Blue	Green	Gold	Orange
Personality Lingo	Connector	Thinker	Planner	Mover
Color Lingo	Blue	Green	Gold	Orange
Personality Dimensions	Blue	Green	Gold	Orange
Insight Learning	Blue	Green	Gold	Orange
Real Colors	Blue	Green	Gold	Orange
Spectrum temperament	Blue	Green	Gold	Orange
Color Code	Blue/White	Red	N/A	Yellow
Herman Brain	Red	Blue	Green	Yellow
Ritburger	Orange	Green	Red	Yellow
Myers-Briggs	ENFJ, INFJ ENFP, INFP	ENTJ, INTJ ENTP, INTP	ESTJ, ISTJ ESFJ, ISFJ	ESFP, ISFP ESTP, ISTP
Keirsey Temperaments	NF	NT	SJ	SP
Keirsey / Bates	Apollonian	Promethean	Epimethean	Dionysian
Keirsey current	Idealist	Rational	Guardian	Artisan
Ancient Greek	Fire	Water	Earth	Air
Carl Jung	Feeling	Thinking	Sensing	Intuition
Seasons	Summer	Winter	Autumn	Spring
Inner Hero	Helper	Thinker	Planner	Doer
Helen Fisher	Estrogen/ Oxytocin	Testosterone	Serotonin	Dopamine

Now, let's get to know both yourself and your customers. We prefer to keep things simple and fun.

CHAPTER 1

'LE FAUT PAS'

Jerry works for a company that produces and sells some of the best skin care 'Crèmes' in the world. She is proud to represent the brand. At the price point the products sell, they are retailed in top end luxury stores. These stores have a very discerning clientele of well heeled customers who are used to superb customer service, from the moment the valets park their cars to the time they finish their shopping.

What the customer does not know and will never be made aware of is that the salespeople in the store are under tremendous and unrelenting pressure. They must produce results and hit targets with low stock levels, constantly changing rules and regulations and an upper management team that is indifferent to bringing in new clients to help the salespeople make their goals.

Just last week Jerry was on product promotion and was handed a sales goal that was more than all the stock she had on the shelves. Ever willing to help the store and her customers, Jerry called her shrinking client list to let them know she had a gift with purchase. She would have their order ready for them when they came in to pick it up or she would gladly deliver it to their home if the customer preferred.

"I'm sorry, I don't have that in stock right now but I can search the system and get it for you…" Jerry said to many of her customers, as the items she needed for them were not in her showcases. "It will take about five business days and I can no longer offer you free delivery because you have not met the minimum dollar amount for free shipping" she said to one of her good clients , Mrs. X. "What do you mean Jerry?" said the customer. "I have shopped with you for many years and you always sent my crème to me with no delivery charge. It is difficult for me to get around with my arthritis. Why charge me now? I spend thousands of dollars a year at your store in all the departments!" "I'm so sorry Mrs. X" said an increasingly demoralized Jerry. "Let me see what I can do to make this better and I will call you right back."

Jerry picked up her client book and walked into the administration office to search for her supervisor. Steven, the supervisor was at his desk and looked pained to see Jerry at the door. "Yes?" he said to Jerry in a tone that was already combative and oozing with condescension. Even before Jerry could speak he then said to her "Should you not be on the floor dealing with customers?" Jerry had dealt with his attitude in times past and today was obviously not going to be an exception. "Steven, I was just wondering if you could make an exception to the delivery charge for Mrs. X's order today as it does not meet the new minimum for complimentary shipping. She is one of my best clients and is already being made to wait for her items as I need to have them sent in from another location." "What is she buying?" he asked Jerry in a tone that was nothing short of imperious. Jerry looked at her sales slip and said "Her order is about $435 dollars and would be more but she just replenished her items last month and does not need more product."

Steven leaned back in his chair and looked at Jerry with cold eyes. "Policy states that the order must be $450 for complimentary shipping and Mrs. X has clearly not met that threshold so the answer is 'No'. So you can either go back and tell her to buy more or charge her the fee."

Jerry looked at him and felt her face become red. "Steven, she has been one of my best clients for several years and sends her friends to me all the time. As a matter of fact she just spent $3,000 last week in the designer department on a dress for her granddaughter's wedding and brought two of the bridesmaids to me for crèmes. Plus she has a hard time getting to the store with her arthritis. It's not going to go over well that we want to charge her a delivery fee!"

"Are you questioning my decision? " asked Steven suddenly sitting up straight in his chair. "We cannot make exceptions for every customer." "No!" he said to a thoroughly demoralized Jerry.

"I will tell her that we have to charge her," said Jerry.

Jerry was beyond frustrated and angry. She knew what the outcome of the call would leave her feeling mortified with embarrassment and shame for having been forced to look petty when the management publically preached that their associates were empowered to deliver the 'Best' in customer service.

Nevertheless, she told herself that she was a loyal employee and went back to her counter to pick up the phone. She dialed the number of Mrs. X and told her the outcome of the discussion with her supervisor had been. As expected, the order was cancelled. Even though Mrs. X was kind to her, Jerry knew that she had lost another customer. There were other shops she could go to get her crèmes that would deliver for free.

Realizing that she was not going to make her goal or her commission that day Jerry tried to put her mind on other things and busied herself trying to make her showcases look full. "Something has to give today," she thought. "I am not going to make my goal and that will go on my file with Human Resources. This will be the third time in the last five months and I will be put to part time or let go for not meeting the targets!" Just then, as she was sinking into despair, Cindy, the daughter of one of her best clients came bounding up to her counter with her latest toddler in tow.

"Oh Jerry!! I am so glad that you are here today!" said the beautiful young woman. "You know my mother's skin so well and I want to get her a gift for her birthday. She talks so highly of you each time she comes back from shopping with you and I am sure that one of your crèmes will make her birthday so wonderful!"

"Let me look at your mother's file Cindy and we can choose something that she will love," said Jerry with delight. "Your mother is such a special person and it is my pleasure to help you make her day something to be remembered." Minutes later a decision had been made and it was agreed that the choice would thrill Cindy's mother.

Jerry went to the till and rang the crème in. It was one of the most expensive crèmes that the brand had but Cindy's mother adored it and always used it. "Well it's expensive but my mother is worth it and I have a gift card that is worth about half the price that I have been saving for just this purpose. This little one here is taking up quite a bit of our income! Here you go!" she said with a huge smile as she thrust the gift card into

Jerry's hand and hugged her child who was becoming uneasy as even the best behaved little children often do.

Jerry looked at the gift card and her heart sank. Cindy could see the look of concern on her face and asked what was the matter. "Cindy, I think your gift card may not apply to this item," she said. "What do you mean Jerry? It's a gift card for this store isn't it?" Cindy questioned, "Can I not use it for my mother's gift? She loves this product like no other." "Let me check for you." Jerry said, "I know that we have made exceptions in the past. I just have to ask my supervisor. I will be right back."

Cindy was made to wait while Jerry went to find Steven, as her toddler was squirming with all his might to get out of her grasp. In the meantime Jerry had tracked down Steven and brought him over to the counter. Jerry introduced Cindy to Steven and made him aware of the relationship that her mother had with her. "Steven, this is Cindy and her mother is having an important birthday. She would like to give her one of her favourite crèmes and use this gift card from the store to pay for half of the cost." The toddler was now going into full struggle to get out of Cindy's arms as Steven looked at the gift card. "We cannot accept this card for use in this transaction. It is for other areas of the store." Steven declared. "But this is all my mother wants from this store for her birthday," said an astonished Cindy who was desperately trying to hold on to her child and becoming increasingly agitated herself. "You mean to tell me I can only use a store card in certain sections of the store???!!!" "That is what it says." declared Steven "I cannot make exceptions for every card that comes in this store."

Jerry was close to tears and Cindy looked equally deflated. "I'm so sorry Cindy" Jerry said softly and dejectedly as the toddler began to wail. "I am too" said Cindy as she packed the gift card back into her purse and hurriedly left the store.

Jerry looked down at the jar of crème that was now sitting on the glass with no owner. She resolved to make a change right there and then. She took a deep breath and walked out from behind the counter and up to Steven who was, as usual chatting idly with another supervisor. "Steven, could I speak with you for a minute please?" she inquired trying not to shake.

"Yes Jerry, what is it now?" Said Steven with a sarcastic tone.

" I am sorry to tell you Steven that you may have to make an 'exception' this time and listen to me when I tell you that I am leaving this store effective immediately! If you can't make exceptions for exceptional customers then don't expect exceptional staff to stay!" With that Jerry left the store and went on to create a new life.

Three months later the store sold to another chain of retailers and Steven was not among those kept to run it. Jerry got a phone call from a headhunter and guess who is handling the customers' needs now!!

CHAPTER 2

WHAT MAKES EACH OF US SPECIAL?

As professionals in the world of retail, you see all types of very different people; from the "Hurry up I'm busy and I need to get this done!" To the "What is this product made of, what's in it?" to "This is too expensive, when will it be on sale?" You see the negotiator, the bargain hunter, the customer who just wants to talk and let's not forget the one who does not talk at all.

You witness your customers come in and out of your stores. You ask yourselves, **"What are they thinking about, what do they want**?" Are they just looking *'The Browser'* or do they really want to buy something *'The Shopper'*? As a retailer, you want your customers to come into your stores to purchase an article or service. However, prior to the purchase of any article for service, there are steps required that we must all know.

It all begins with the first questions that we hope are going through your minds and coming out of your mouths, *"How can I help*?" How can I give this customer what they really need? How do I make a connection with this person? We know that these questions are going through your minds, all within seconds of that customer coming into your line of sight. Yet, we have gone into stores, restaurants and the 'so called' service provider is sitting behind the cash register counter, playing with their cell phone or simply staring into a void.

There is an adventure here to be had. We can enjoy the adventure by simply observing customers as they shop around in your stores.

Let them get comfortable, and let them go in the direction they need to go. We are all aware of this, having done exactly that on so many occasions. We have all gone into stores, just walked around and watched, watched other customers doing business, employees doing their job and the interaction between them. Quite fascinating when you think of it.

What is even more enjoyable is the first steps of interaction, just like one person approaching another to ask them out on a first date. Pay attention the next time you are in a store and a sales clerk comes to help. Picture them getting ready to ask you out on a date. Your reaction will change, you may even want to be defensive, but don't be, it is simply someone doing his or her job.

What many have tried, was to change the behaviour of the customer the moment they first interact with the sales person. Whether it be a friend, loved one, child or another customer. **Yes**! We have all tried at one point in our lives, with epic failures we might add. We stood there wondering what happened. Why are they so upset? Why did we lose that customer or friend? Why did they leave screaming and yelling telling us, **"You don't understand me"** or **"I can't talk to you"**? Unfortunately, due to our lack of understanding of the other person or persons, we keep committing this unintended offense over and over again.

Philosophers have been pondering over human behaviour for centuries. Interestingly enough human behaviour is being consistently rediscovered each and every day with new perspectives, theories, etc.

With various numbers of personality systems out there, which we briefly have shown, what do they all mean? Are there clear and precise answers to what makes people do what they do? Unfortunately there is nothing that is 100% clear when it comes to human behavior.

What we are providing is an expanded picture of what people may do. For example, we can believe the behaviour of a person who is high ORANGE on the spectrum can be that of an impulse buyer, quick to make a decision. A high GREEN will seek detail prior to making any type of decision and so on. More detail on other colours to come.

Everyone on this planet, over seven billion of us, have very different ways of saying what we would like to say, hoping that our message is understood on the receiving end of the discussion. However, the reality is, it's all an interpretation of your message; two people who are very different will see and hear the same message, however, they will interpret it very differently.

Within the world of retail, we ask ourselves **"Will they be buying or browsing"**, **"How much will they spend"** and **"What do they want?"** There is very little difference if you think about it, to being in a relationship. When your significant other seems to be quiet, we ask them **"Is everything all right? Have I done something to offend you?"** They may simply want time to reflect on their day, or are trying to figure out a problem in their head. The unknown is enough to make you go crazy.

Incredibly, all this is going through our minds so rapidly that we make it a daily ritual, a repetitious habit. We show up to work, put on our uniforms, set up our workstations and open the doors, anticipating what we call the customer to come in. We start the routine over and over again each and every day.

'**What if**' we were to provide you with a different way of seeing things, a more practical, more fun, more intellectual or concrete way of seeing your potential clients? Imagine having a relationship with everyone that comes through those doors, a relationship so secretive that the client doesn't even know it's happening. All they know is that they are enjoying your company. You help them feel good about themselves, it lets them feel as if they are walking into an old friend's home and to a wonderfully warm and memorable welcome. The customer will leave your store wanting to come back for more.

The simple fact is that when you feel recognized as an individual, you feel significant.

How would **YOU** feel at the end of each and every day if you felt recognized?

Here is another big question, what would the management team think of you after such a day, a week, a year? Being recognized, take a moment and imagine such a day. Doesn't that thought bring warmth inside of you? Would you not want to get up each and every day and want to go to work and meet with your favorite clients? **Yes!**

Wouldn't you want this to become your permanent way of being, acting and behaving with every potential client coming near you? The place where you will build a relationship. Hmmmm!?

We are guaranteed you are saying to yourself, "How do you plan to teach me all that? Good luck."

This adventure begins with first knowing who we are: knowing our personality traits, our temperament. How can we move forward and understand others if we are not clear as to who we are. Our disposition is coded in our DNA, it remains there throughout our lives whether you like it or not. Knowing and understanding your personality style are key factors in this journey we are about to take together. When we understand others, it helps us to recognize our similarities and differences in this wonderful world and address each and every customer in a fashion that is engaging and appealing.

These powerful insights will help you to work with your potential customer and give them the feeling of shopping with a friend. You will create numerous relationships and build a great clientele of people that will want to keep coming and coming, just to come and say hello to YOU.

Let us share this little story with you. *A colleague and I had not seen each other in many months, it was a pleasure to see him again. Standing in the lobby of a hotel, we contemplated as to where we should go for dinner. There were a number of fabulous restaurants nearby, however, at that point it was irrelevant as to where we went, as we knew we would be talking for hours.*

With a quick turn of the head we noticed the restaurant in the hotel, it looked inviting, modern, fresh but most important there were smiles on the employees faces. Our first reaction was, "this looks just fine." We weren't looking for something specific to eat, nothing big or heavy, just something light and simple and great tasting.

We walked to the entrance, where a wonderful young lady named Mary greeted us. Mary was a tall woman with a radiant smile. Her face was streaming of joy and passion for everyone in her presence. With such an authentic personality a welcome like no other was given by Mary, like you would give when meeting up with a long lost friend.

"Will you be dining with us this evening or simply enjoying a refreshment at the bar gentlemen?" Mary said with a smile.

"We will be having dinner this evening" I responded with a nod of the head.

Walking ahead of us she brought us to our table and turned, "How is this? You get a great view of the entire restaurant and surrounding. You can also see our Sushi Chef at work." Her appearance, composure, body language and vocabulary was not something that had been rehearsed. She was not following a script that had been handed to her to memorize. Mary was engaged in the discussion, looking for us to join in and chat. We felt welcomed and appreciated as people, not just another customer.

Paul leaned slightly over to read her nametag, and before he could say anything she said, "Mary, you can simply call me Mary."

"This is perfect Mary," Paul said with a responsive smile. "Thank you, and would there be somewhere I can put my coat?"

Mary helped him with his coat, folding it over her forearm, "We have a very secure closet over there on the side, only the staff are permitted in. Let me bring it there and return with your portion of the tag on the hanger. It will simplify the search if I can't retrieve it for you. I hope that will work for you, if not, I can put it over the chair next to you, either way is just fine with me."

Paul responded in the same pleasant fashion presented to him, "Perfect, the closet will do."

"Let me bring this to the closet and I will return with water and the menus. Would either of you gentlemen like a beverage?" she said, always keeping eye contact with either Paul or myself.

"Perrier please" I said, "for myself also," replied Paul

"Gentlemen, I will be right back" and she headed off to the closet.

Returning in minutes with a large bottle of Perrier and two glasses on a tray and menus in her other hand, she put the menus on the next empty table and brought the tray down and poured our drinks.

The service was exceptional, the food was delightful. Mary made it a point to make sure that every single detail of our short stay was memorable, making it a wonderful experience.

Here is what we also observed, Mary treated each and every customer who walked in with the same grateful attitude and the response was always returned with a smile. Some were actual return customers and they remembered her name, talking with her like long lost friends, letting Mary know how well things were going. When speaking with everyone, she made it a point to look at them, adding that important little factor that means so much to everyone, **'Look at me when you are talking to me'**.

We will share these short stories throughout the book with you to bring you   some great life experiences we have had some that we would like to forget, but that can be used as a great learning lesson for all of us.

As we proceed, our stories will include details as to the primary and secondary colours of the individuals in the stories to add perspective to the reality and simplicity of their temperament styles. We also encourage you to sit and reflect on your own experience, good or bad, and ask yourself, **'Would I return to that store, restaurant or service provider?'**

It is also important to bring forward an element that will be recurring in this book. **'Feeling'**. If there is something that we have noticed in our years of experience is the concept of **'feeling'** - how the individual felt as they entered a store, how they felt as they were being served. We are all emotional beings, however, there are some of us who live on a plane of **logic**, leaving little or no room for emotion, nevertheless it is very much present in all our lives.

We are all aware that good service goes a long way, but truly understanding world-class service will bring you to places you can barely imagine, and will have your customers wanting more of YOU. Unfortunately many assume that providing world-class service requires a lot of effort and work. Unfortunately, you have been mislead, IT'S EASY!

Ask yourself, how would you feel if a customer came into your store and requested you and only you because of how 'YOU' made them feel special?

Here is a great example: *There was a young clerk in a furniture store, limited in his education but very well schooled in the world of 'doing just a little more* *than expected'. This young clerk made it a daily ritual to ensure the cleanliness of his section in the store, assist others without being asked, stay a little longer when customers were still in the store and arrive earlier upon delivery of new stock, to prepare for the displays. Diligent, assiduous to the core he was, the price he had to pay was to be ridiculed by his fellow employees, consistently being call "the bosses pet, the company suck up", etc.*

He kept doing this day after day, without any expectations of grandness or big promotions, he loved what he did and did it with passion.

One rainy day, an elderly lady was standing out in front of the store, taking shelter from the rain. After a few moments the young man opened the door and politely asked the women if all was Ok!

"Everything is fine young man, thank you for asking. I am waiting for my son to come and pick me up. I let him know I was going to be in front of this store so that he can easily find me." She said with a shiver that made her whole body shake.

The young man was well aware of the current store policy 'No loitering at store entrances'. The company wanted a clear doorway for customers to come through. The young man did not let this deter him from letting this cold old lady in and out of the rain, he had a plan. "Madame, can I suggest that you come in from the cold and wait inside, with our big windows you will easily see your son coming and he will see you."

"But I'm not shopping son," the woman said.

The young man held her arm gently and said, "You can window shop!" with a smile.

They walked into the store, the young man pulled a chair from the dining room table which was on display and asked her to be seated. As she sat, he pulled out another chair and sat next to her and a conversation was struck. The rest of the staff stood in the back, staring, talking amongst each other saying things that I will let your imagination think of. You know the kind.

About 15 minutes had gone by when a vehicle pulled up in front of the store. The gentlemen driving was surely looking for someone, looking up and down the street. He then looked directly in the store window and noticed his mother, in deep discussion with a young man at the dining room table on display. He stepped out of the car, came into the store and said "Hello mother, are we shopping today?"

She turned to her son and with a smile "No! I was window shopping today and I also had the best assistant I have had in my entire life." As she made a hand gesture in the direction of the young man.

He looked at the young man and asked, "What is your name son?"

"Eric sir, my name is Eric", standing with his hand out in a pleasant greeting.

As the gentlemen shook Eric's hand he said, "Thank you so much for keeping my mother company, I hope it didn't take you away from your work."

With confidence Eric responded, "Sir, I was blessed to have had this short period of time with this wonderful lady. You can say this is my work, for everyone to have a great store experience."

"Your mother helped make my day a day to remember. Thank you Madame for taking the time out of your day to spend with me," said Eric as he held her hand in his.

The gentlemen walked his mother to the car and they waved goodbye.

You would think that would be the end of the story, but with world-class service comes world-class rewards. Eric was not aware who these people were; all that mattered to Eric was that he had made a new friend, this wonderful elderly woman.

One day a Vice President from the corporate office came into the store, and was standing in the manager's office having a very serious talk. Corporate VP's very seldom came to the store, they kept busy in their offices. The staff were nervous, as the custom was when corporate representative showed up, no good could come of it.

As the discussion kept going, the manager pointed in Eric's direction.

The VP walked out of the office and marched in his direction, "I hear great things about you Eric, I am Donald C. Edwards, Vice President of Public Relations. We have had a very specific and peculiar request from a very special customer of ours." Donald said as he was shaking Eric's hand.

"Let me get right to the point. Our customer is the head of a very prominent family here in the US, however, they have just purchased a home in England and would like our store to refurnish the entire house. Let me add that this is no ordinary home. It stands on many acres of land, has 13 bedrooms, 3 main dining rooms, multiple bathrooms and so on, you get the picture."

Eric was not clear as to why he was being provided all this information, and so he asked, "Sir, I am not clear as to why or how I could be of service to this family *in their new home in England? Believe me, I would be honored to be of assistance but I'm unclear as to how."*

"Eric, that is a great question and I am glad to hear you would like to help. Our usual practice for such cases is that a member of the management staff would assist the customer at the local store, unfortunately this was not acceptable for our customer. She had made it very clear to us that the only person from our store that would be setting foot in her home would be you!" Donald was looking directly at Eric waiting for a response.

Eric was more confused than ever, "I do not understand Sir, I am sure there are many more qualified individuals who would be more than happy to take on this task, especially those in England."

Donald was quick with his response, "I do not agree Eric, let me share this with you. This customer told me a very interesting story. She was overwhelmed by the service of a young man in our store called Eric, as he not only invited her in to the store but also kept her company and made her feel very special. She made it clear that this young man was going to be responsible for the refurnishing of their entire home in England and strongly suggested he reestablish himself in England to manage the store."

Eric had to take a step back, he could not believe what he was hearing, Donald continued "Eric, your kindness and honesty was not only noticed by the mother but by her son, who is owner of one of the largest iron companies in the world, Mr. Andrew Carnegie." Donald kept on. "They have been a valued customers of ours for many years and when this story came to us at the presidents level, we had no hesitation to acknowledge their request and come to meet with you and see for ourselves who you are."

Donald posed for a moment, looking down at first then back up at Eric, "I am honored to say that you have gone over and beyond what is asked of you. May I ask why you work this way Eric?"

Eric stood erect and prepared to answer this question with pride, "Sir, I don't see people coming in and out of our stores just as customers, I see them as part of my extended family. I treat them the way I would treat any member of my family, with care and respect, allowing them the time they need with me. No customer of mine should feel like they are a burden or a waste of time, they should feel great to come into our stores. This is not a job Sir, this is who I am. I just happen to have the good fortune to be employed here."

Donald was not sure as to how to respond, he did what any family member would do, he reached over and gave Eric a hug, "You are an amazing young man and I would be honored if I can contact our customer and let her know that you have taken the manager's position in our store in England and will be there to help them in their new home."

"The honor is all mine Sir, and thank you," Eric said humbly.

This is a true story that took place back in the 1850's in the United States of America (USA). Eric not only managed the store in England but also returned to the USA to become Vice President of Customer Service. Gifts of kindness are never forgotten, we all have great examples, but sadly we get so wrapped up in the negative stories that we forget how easy it is to be kind.

We wrote this book to provide you with tools to bring a positive twist in your retail world. Enjoy the adventure.

Are you ready?!!!

CHAPTER 3

'YOU'

The world knows that every snowflake is different, even though they all have characteristics that are very similar. Snowflakes come in a variety of sizes and shapes. Complex shapes emerge as the flake moves through differing temperature and humidity regimes, so that individual snowflakes are unique in structure. The same is true of human beings, we are also unique and different. Each and every one of us are remarkable individuals, but we possess many commonalities.

Are you ready and willing to explore them?

Since there are over 7 billion people on the planet, it stands to reason that there may be billions of variations in personalities. Now, you may have noticed by now that there are similarities in the natural tendencies of yourself and others. When conducting workshops, we ask participants, "Who here is spontaneous, who here is organized, romantic, etc." Never have we had only one person in a large group raise their hand. There are traits that are very common with each and every one of us.

We also need to add that every one of us may change our behaviour based on the circumstance we are in at the moment. For example, our behaviour may become very structured and organized when a member of management comes to our workstation, when a task is required we set out to be organized to complete the job. We become relaxed when we are with close friends and family, we let ourselves get closer to each other, leaving emotions free to be enjoyed. We become focused when looking for that special something for a loved one, an anniversary, a special event, we are driven to find something special.

In many cases we find that perhaps you or someone you know was not able to truly **"Be themselves"** for one reason or another, trying to impersonate another person, being told to behave a specific way because your way was embarrassing them. You work in an environment that does not appeal to you, it may be a good job but you just cannot put your heart and soul into it, there is something missing. We then turn on ourselves and find fault with who we are, thinking that we must be the problem, we must be the cause of the issues. We think there is something truly wrong with '**Me**'.

There is nothing wrong with who you are. You just have not found who you truly are. You may not be aware, but, you are in a searching pattern. Doesn't it feel like a never ending revolving door, never knowing when this constant whirl-wind will end?

Let's put an end to this internal conflict. Let's start having fun with who we are. Let's learn of our full potential and apply these 'new found' concepts to our lives.

CHAPTER 4

WHY USE COLOURS?

Within this chapter, you will discover the characteristics of the colours we have used to profile your personalities.

We live in a world of colours. Colours are all around us. Colours are in our dreams and in our inspirations, and in every single thing around us. We will use this wonderful tool to **'Colourize yourself'**.

You will be able to identify yourself within the four colours to be discussed. Your colours permit you to recognize people around you, family, friends and customers. You will understand your values, strengths and needs, and you will understand how you need to be treated to live a fulfilling life. You will also learn how best you communicate and begin discovering your authentic 'Self'.

So why would we all want to know what our colours are? Self-identity has been a fundamental factor in many personality behaviors, so what we provide you with is the simplest and easiest of ways to see yourself and identify the behaviors in others. Understanding others permits us all to speak and communicate on a common playing field, removing self-imposed barriers such as **'I can't talk to this person'** or **'Here comes Mr. so and so, I'm out of here'**, creating that link you feel that is missing.

We will guide you in first identifying what your primary colors are. What drives you. Are you action oriented, passionate for the well being of others, organized or in search of the unknown? Understanding this will give you a picture of what is important to you, what takes priority in your life, such as: "Do you prefer to have fun rather than doing the same old routine or do you prefer reading a good book to the company of others?

The challenge we have in self-identification is getting away from what has been said to us in regards to what we should or should not like, so we come to the conclusion that whatever has been programmed in our brain must be true to have a productive life, to fit in.

When you are told **'You should act this way'**, it is the furthest thing from the truth. Identifying one's self will open your eyes to **'Why have I been doing this all my life, or I hate this or this is not me, this is my mother, etc'**. Being appreciative of one's self is the doorway to appreciating and understanding those around us. So ask yourself, how can you value anyone else if you do not see the value in yourself?

We have struggled in our own lives with self-identity and the results of our findings we know will bring clarity to the world within and around you.

CHAPTER 5

IDENTIFYING YOUR COLOURS

Who is Blue?
Your Strength is Authenticity

You seek to express the inner you. Authenticity and honesty are valued above all other characteristics. You enjoy close relationships with those you love and possess a strong spirituality in your nature. Making a difference in the world is easy for you because you cultivate the potential in yourself and in others. Keep in mind that a person can still be considered to be Blue dominant without having all of the characteristics listed.

Caretaker - Nurturing, sensitive to the needs of others. Usually, the first one to notice that someone isn't feeling well or needs help and will want to offer assistance. Frequently puts the needs of others before themselves.

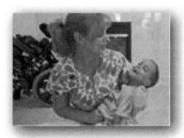

Optimistic - Looks on the bright side of things. Likely to be the one who sees "The light at the end of the tunnel" during a crisis. Motivates and encourages others.

Passionate - Devoted to and intoxicated by their interests. Whether it's collecting antiques, motivating a team, or building a relationship, they throw heart and soul into it. Can be very dramatic.

Enthusiastic - Speaks kindly and compliments freely. Expressive, persuasive, stimulating, and inspirational. Lives to have everyone around them happy and comfortable. Often feels it is their duty to cheer up others or provide motivation.

Imaginative - Creative, expressive, and inspired. May be drawn towards art, music, or drama. Possibly will write and speak with poetic flair or use metaphors. Sees possibility, hope, and future potential.

Cause Oriented - May volunteer their time and get involved in causes such as recycling, helping victims of violent crimes, feeding the hungry, raising consciousness, self-improvement, spiritual growth, and so on.

Needs to be Unique - Strives for genuine self-expression and their own identity. Although they may be good at modifying their behaviour like a chameleon to fit the needs of the person they are relating to at the moment, they aspire to be unique in their own way. BLUES are able to spot, and like to bring out, the best in others. They will take any opportunity to bolster someone else's self-esteem or acknowledge others' uniqueness or talents.

Cooperative Rather than Competitive - Encourages team-building rather than "may the best man win" attitude. Good group or team participant. Enjoys the friendship and camaraderie of working together on a project or goal.

People Oriented - Accepting of differences, friendly, and affirming. Relates well with people. Makes an effort to connect with and acknowledge others. Most every decision made is determined by how it will affect the people involved. Promotes growth and development of others.

Peacemaker - Most comfortable when everyone is getting along with each other. When conflicts arise, can become distracted from work or even affected physically. Will go to great lengths to restore harmony, even if it means holding quiet their own point of view for the moment. The relationship is more important than being right.

Mediator - BLUES enjoy harmony and a peaceful atmosphere. Family frictions, co-worker conflicts or other demanding disputes can be very distracting for them, even if the conflict does not involve them. They may try to mediate, "You have a good point, and you do too, can't we come to some sort of agreement?" BLUES try to foster collaboration and team spirit whenever possible.

Who is Gold?
Your Strength is Duty

You value order and cherish the traditions of home and family. Generous and parental by nature, you show you care by helping everyone do the right thing. Steadfastness and loyalty are your trademarks, and you provide for and support the structure of society. To disregard responsibility of any kind never occurs to you.

Prepared - Thinks ahead to be ready in advance. Uncomfortable putting things off until the last minute. Will carry backups just in case. Usually has a contingency plan.

Loves to Plan - Can see every step that needs to be taken to reach the goal. Is able to realistically determine timelines. Good at linear thinking, one thing leads to another. Often has checklists to follow on projects.

Detail Oriented - Notices particulars that others may never think of. Sees the trees in the forest as well as the bark, bugs, and leaves.

Punctual - Makes every effort to be on time and appreciates it when others are also.

Strong Sense of Duty - Enjoys being useful and responsible. Service oriented, very helpful, and dependable. Reliable, supports family, organization, and community. Can be counted on to implement, execute, and follow through.

Belief in Policies - Supports procedures and rules. Most likely of all the colour styles to drive the speed limit or even under it. Implements, administers, and supports requirements.

Values Family Traditions - Usually likes to celebrate holidays the way they have been done for generations. If they own a family business they tend to want to pass it down to an offspring. Enjoys family-related gatherings: may even plan them.

Conscientious - Does not litter and is bothered when others do. Tries to conserve resources and keep things tidy. Is trustworthy and honest, loyal to spouse. Has a strong work ethic. Hard on themselves if they don't follow through.

Conservative and Stable - Predictable and consistent. Likes having a sense of security or safety net. Values order and the status quo. Chooses to save for a rainy day instead of spending in the moment.

Well-Organized - Comfortable within an orderly, consistent environment. "A place for everything and everything in its place" is a motto that many GOLDS try to live by at home as well as at work. Has a knack for knowing the most efficient place and method for storing or arranging things.

Strong "Should" and "Should Not" - Knows the difference between right and wrong. Is aware of what would be appropriate in various circumstances. Gets upset or concerned when other people violate customary norms.

Most Comfortable with a Structured Environment - Likes to know what to expect and what is expected from them. It puts them at ease to know who is in authority and what the rules are so they can follow them.

Guy L Moisan & Doug Atkinson

Who is Orange?
Your Strength is Skillfulness

You have a zest for life and a desire to test the limits best describe your nature. You take pride in being highly skilled in a variety of fields and need freedom to take immediate action. You prefer a hand-on approach to problem solving, and a direct line of reasoning creates the excitement and immediate results you admire. You are a master negotiator; adventure is your middle name.

Energetic - High need for mobility. Likes to get movement somehow throughout the day. Usually enjoys recreational activities, for example: skiing, boating, dirt biking, skateboarding, dancing, and so on. May be drawn to competitive sports.

Desires Change - Enjoys variety, flexibility, and resourcefulness. This could include many aspects of life such as jobs, projects, relationships, and environment. Questions the status quo, expects others to adapt to situational requirements. Enjoys surprises and will take chances.

Playful - Quick-witted and humorous, likes to bring fun to a situation. Can be flirtatious. Is interested in the process of reaching a goal as much as achieving it.

Master Negotiator - Charming, enjoys making a deal. "No" is often interpreted as "maybe." Tries to find a way to accomplish desires.

Natural Entertainer - Can be a bit flamboyant. May call attention to themselves by the way they dress, act, or speak. Likes to have the interest of others. May give extravagant gifts and takes pleasure in seeing the reaction of the receiver.

Pushes Boundaries - Tests limits, natural non-conformist and risk taker. May live on the edge. Seeks excitement. Can get bogged down by red tape and rules. Many times can find loopholes in the system and may bend the rules if necessary to accomplish goals.

Accepts Challenges - Derives pleasure in solving problems. Thrives on competition and likes adapting to last-minute changes. Able to troubleshoot and act in a crisis. May get involved in situations just to see if they can be successful where others have failed.

Impulsive and Spontaneous - Likes to leave options open so that they have the freedom to choose. May easily get distracted from task at hand if interruptions aren't kept to a minimum. Likes to live in the moment; may arrange life to include making on-the-spot decisions.

"Just Do It" - Finds planning tedious. Makes decisions and takes action quickly. Hates to wait. Wants to "get the show on the road." May also change their mind as instantly as they made it up.

Appreciates Immediate Feedback - Delayed feedback is almost meaningless. Prefers giving as well as getting straight responses at once, instead of waiting.

Most Productive in Non-Structured Environments - Likes to be able to kick off shoes and be comfortable. Enjoys an environment that is changing and unpredictable.

Self-Confident - Takes initiative. May jump in and take over leadership role if others are perceived as ineffective or hesitant.

Who is Green?
Your Strength is Knowledge

You feel best about yourself when solving problems, especially when your ingenious ideas are recognized. You seek to express yourself through your ability to be an expert in everything, and your idea of a great day is to use your know-how to create solutions. You are complex individualist with great analytical ability. Although you do not express your emotions openly, you do experience deep feelings.

Problem Solver - Diligently works at finding a way to accomplish the task at hand. Has a tremendous amount of tenacity for figuring out solutions and enjoys the challenge.

"Why?" Mentality - Wants to know the reasons why things must be done a certain way. "Because we've always done it that way" is not a good reason. Desires to know the logic or theory behind things. Very philosophical, interested in the "why" of human behaviour. Inquisitive

Very Complex - Abstract, theoretical, conceptual. Global thinker, looks at the big picture. Uses systematic approaches to situations or activities, including personal relationships.

Standard-Setters - Visionary, futurist, idea person, insightful. Often an inventor, technician, scientist, or engineer. Establishes new protocols and systems, especially for technological advances, that may influence society as a whole. The Einstein's and Edison's.

Cool, Calm, Collected - Maintains composure in situations where others may become outwardly emotional. Considers expression of feelings, such as crying, as getting in the way of relationships instead of enhancing them. Looks at the principles involved in the situation; can work without harmony. Decides objectively. Firm-minded and can give criticism when appropriate.

Intellectual - Can never know enough. Constantly seeking information. Enjoys investigating matters further. Many Greens have a rather expansive vocabulary - know a tremendous number of "big words" and how to pronounce and use them.

Work Is Play and Play Is Work - Enjoys work so much it may be considered play. Can find "socializing" taxing unless interacting with someone sharing similar interests. Greens are often misunderstood as children because of their inclination towards solo activities.

Need for Independence and Private Time - Seeks autonomy. Doesn't necessarily enjoy or see the value in teamwork. Usually prefers to work alone. Works best without constant direction or coaching. Likes to be able to try new ways outside the norm.

Driven by Competence - Proficient and capable, feels rewarded when a job is done well. Strives for expertise in field or areas of interest. Measurable success is motivating.

Perfectionist - Explores all aspects before making a decision. Takes pride in getting it right the first time and every time.

Analytical - Naturally investigative, able to find flaws and imperfections. Critical thinker - does not take things at face value. Diagnostic, systematic.

I do not know what I may appear to the world, but to myself I seem to have been only like a boy playing on the seashore, and diverting myself in now and then finding a smoother pebble or a prettier shell than ordinary, whilst the great ocean of truth lay all undiscovered before me.
— Isaac Newton

Approaches Interpersonal Relationships in a Logical Manner - Can find it cumbersome to keep up with social expectations. Usually doesn't chitchat about personal matters. Speaks for a purpose, not simply to keep up social ties. May seek "formulas" for personal relationships.

CHAPTER 6

YOUR CUSTOMERS

The approach to each spectrum, with clear expectations and results:

How to talk to a BLUE?

When a BLUE listens, it's more than just mere words they are listening for. It is looking in the persons eyes, trying to see and feel what the other is trying to communicate. They are trying to assess what they see, hear and feel in the communication. It is of great importance to be aligned with the person they are communicating with. If the connection or alignment is not made or clear to the BLUE, there is a tendency to reject the discussion and interpret the message as insincere.

Here is a good example. "BLUES" will try to get a sense of the explanation or topic of the speaker. They will trying to observe the benefits of the discussion. If they feel the person is honest and sincere and truly cares for others, they open up all of their senses and give their undivided attentions to the person. The BLUE person will create a relationship as the other speaker continues their discussion.

Those who have negative views, May see a BLUE as:

Bleeding heart	Soft, pushover	Easily duped	Stuck in the past
Fawning	Too tender-hearted	Hopelessly naive	Too touchy-feely
Overly emotional	Too trusting	Smothering	

Others who have negative views are often individuals who have BLUE as their palest colour and they do not understand you. The key to having positive and supportive relationships is understanding and appreciating differences. Having a positive perceptions of others will contribute to your success and their success.

How to talk to a GOLD?

A GOLD listens for details. In order. They can lose their train of thought if the conversation is interrupted or the person speaks off target. They do not want to fill in the blanks. GOLDS listen for responsibility. They listen for the purpose of gathering information so they know what their part is. They pay attention and ask themselves, "What is my duty? What should I do with the information?"

GOLDS are concerned with whether something is right or wrong. They are listening to decide the correctness of the speaker's intentions as well as their status within the given context. The more they are able to determine the appropriateness of an interaction or response, the more comfortable they are in conversing.

Those who have negative views May see a GOLD as:

Bossy	Controlling	Dull, boring	Judgmental
Opinionated	Predictable	Rigid	Stubborn
System-bound	Unimaginative	Uptight	

Others who have negative views are often individuals who have GOLD as their palest colour and they do not understand you. The key to having positive and supportive relationships is understanding and appreciating differences. Having positive perceptions of others will contribute to your success and their success.

How to talk to an ORANGE?

ORANGES listen for entertainment, impact, relevance and usefulness. Unless you are incredibly engaging or reveal immediately how the information you are conveying is useful to an ORANGE, they may lose interest, especially if your communication is lengthy. If you fail to stimulate or keep their interest, they will do it themselves, making connections to what you are saying so they can in turn tell you a colorful story of something that happened to them. Their minds can whirl a mile-a-minute as they playfully hop from subject to subject.

They also try to figure out the motive of the person speaking. What do they want, need or expect from me? They do this almost simultaneously as they look for opportunities for themselves. They want to be able to take action with what is said, be it to share a quick joke, seize a challenge, or perform some feat. They listen in the present and process contextually, usually not linking so much to the past or distant future, but instead figuring out what they can do with the information in the moment.

Those who have negative views May see an ORANGE as:

Disobeys the rules	Flakey, goofs off too much	Indecisive	Irresponsible
Manipulative	Not able to stay on task	Not to be trusted	Obnoxious
Resists closure	Scattered, cluttered	Uncontrollable	

Others who have negative views are often individuals who have ORANGE as their palest colour and they do not understand you. The key to having positive and supportive relationships is understanding and appreciating differences. Having positive perceptions of others will contribute to your success and their success.

How to talk to a GREEN?

GREENS listen for information and want to know the purpose for the communication. Often, they assume the communicator has approached them to solve a problem or to exchange necessary or intriguing material. They tune out redundancy, extreme emotion, and subjects that are of little interest to them. They seem to automatically click into data gathering and concept or strategy formation. They focus so intensely on thinking about and processing (then reprocessing from several different approaches) the "data" presented that they regularly miss out on the additional messages supplied by non-verbal communication such as tonality, body language and facial expressions. You may be sharing to gain empathy and instead they are concentrating on solving your challenge, offering little or no outward signs of compassion, while all the while in their minds they are demonstrating the ultimate compassion by taking the time to solve your problem.

Those who have negative views May see a GREEN as:

Afraid to open up	Eccentric, weird	Arrogant	Emotionally controlled
Cool, aloof, unfeeling	Heartless, ruthless	Critical, fault finding	Intellectual snob
Doesn't care	Lacking mercy	Devaluing relational aspects	Unfair, unrealistic

Others who have negative views are often individuals who have GREEN as their palest colour and they do not understand you. The key to having positive and supportive relationships is understanding and appreciating differences. Having positive perceptions of others will contribute to your success and their success.

CHAPTER 7

YOU AND YOUR CUSTOMERS

O ur approach is to give value, appreciation and importance to the customer - How to do that?

If I am a BLUE.

Being a BLUE gives you the ability to adapt to the styles of others. We will provide you with a few suggestions to assist you in the task of listening for a BLUE. Without a doubt you are already very well aware of your own communication habits and the effect they have on others. You are driven to be flexible and want to learn more in regards to helping or assisting others. Let's build who you are together, this is easy and fun for you.

Being Objective: When speaking with a potential client, you read too much between the lines. When you notice that you have taken a comment personally, pause for a moment. Attach the meaning you have linked to what the other has said to your thought and ask 'Why?' have I joined this thought to this discussion. Some customers may be making comments that are directed to the product and/or store, you only happen to be the candidate who will receive the feedback as 'Negative or Positive'.

Example; Jessica is a most valued customer at store X, however, most of the staff fear having to deal with her based on her abruptness with the staff. Whenever she comes into the store, the perception is that she is very difficult to deal with. Once this judgment has been put in place within the store culture, no matter who is working, this customer is deemed to be 'Bad news'. Do not let your feelings take control of what you are hearing, let the actions speak for themselves. Listen to your customers.

Ensure that your thought and the discussion match, that they are in tune with each other. What was it in the delivery of the message that brought you to that thought in question? Give the benefit of the doubt to the speaker, it may get clear as they continue, don't shut them out to quickly. Pay attention to your intuition and old habitual thinking patterns. Be open to the gift of feedback; be resourceful with what you learn.

Speak Up: Say something before you get to the point of disconnection. If the message is unclear, **ASK**. It's OK to be a little more direct. Your potential client will appreciate you wanting more information so that you can serve them better.

Difference between Politeness and Interest: Notice if others are actually interested in what you have to say. You may be faced with a client who is in a rush but will not say anything, simply give you a vague look. You probably do the same thing when you have other things on your mind and feel the discussion is not adding value to you and your day.

BLUES see themselves as:

Affirming	Romantic	Caretaker	Spiritual
Compassionate	Sympathetic	Empathetic	Trusting
Great communicator	Unselfish	Idealistic	Warm
Liking to please	Willing to work tirelessly for a cause	Promoter of growth and well being	

If I am a GOLD.

Being a GOLD means you are generally respectful and responsible in most areas of your life. This is also frequently true when it comes to communication. If GOLD is your dominant colour, you'll most likely size-up a situation for what would be most appropriate before responding. However, as you are well aware, not everyone shares the same ideals for what is appropriate. Therefore, conflicts can arise. One of the best ways to show consideration for yourself and others is to appreciate each individual's unique style. Instead of trying to convince others that your way is the right way, use the following suggestions to enhance communication and promote alliances.

Have Patience: When people talk in different directions and do ten things at once or don't stick to the agenda, be open minded about their communication styles. This is especially true if you are a listener or the one that has approached them for something you need.

Consider Other Options: GOLDS have a tendency to judge very quickly whether a person's actions are "right" or "wrong" at the onset of a conversation. Pay attention to whether or not you are missing the whole point of the discussion because you got stuck on something that you decided was "wrong" at the beginning of the interaction.

Practice Peripheral Listening: Instead of zoning right in on the details, practice discerning the concept or big picture. Let your customer provide you with the details. Take the time for the customer to tell their stories, if not, you risk losing them forever.

Accept Others: Unless you are in a position to supervise others and it is your job to correct their actions, when their values are not in line with yours, it can be fruitless and irritating to try to change them. Know that others have different skills and values than you, and *different* does not mean *wrong*. Your way may not be the 'Right way' for that situation.

Give It a Break: Remember... you are not the general manager of the universe. Be aware of how hard you are driving yourself and others. Take the weight of the world off your shoulders. Relax a little and realize there are just some things that don't have to be perfect.

GOLDS see themselves as:

Always having a view	Decisive	Dependable	Efficient
Executive type	Firm	Goal oriented	Good planner
Good at sorting	Good at weeding out	Orderly, neat	Organized
Punctual	Realistic	Security-minded	Stable

If I am an ORANGE.

Being an ORANGE, you seek entertainment, impact, relevance and usefulness. You look for a discussion which is engaging, need to receive immediate information or you will disengage and quickly, especially if the communication is lengthy. You require stimulation to keep your interest and if that is not reached in your discussion you will find a way to do so. You think of so many things at one time. You require fun in your life, make it a game.

Be Aware of How You are Coming Across: You may want to "tell it like it is," but some people need to have it wrapped in a nice package. While you might not care about certain things, others do. If it is important to you to be heard, modify your speech to fit the patterns used by your listener.

Wait for a Response before Proceeding: A pause does not equal a 'yes'. Give people time to think. Your mind may run a mile a minute, but others may prefer to plan before taking action. A customer may want to read the information prior to doing the purchase, if that time is not provided, you may have lost them.

Identify Others' Requirements: Some people simply cannot listen until you acknowledge them. Notice if that's the case. Pay attention to whether the listener wants more information or not. Be prepared to take an extra minute. A minute spent now can save you several later.

Notice When You Are Exaggerating: If you embellish too much, too often, people will not believe you anymore and will try to second-guess you. It can be fun to add some colour to your conversations but be aware of the response of others. You might want to save your best stories for those that you know will appreciate them.

When Listening to Others Keep Your Mind Focused: Remember, not everyone can switch gears as quickly as you can, or even wants to. Curb the impulse to interrupt those you know find it distracting.

Pause before Making a Commitment: Think past the moment to check and see if you can really follow through. Set up ways to remember the promises you made yesterday.

Recognize Others: Others need praise as much as you do. Find out how they like to receive it and give it to them their way.

Use Softeners When Making Requests or Giving Directions: Using "please" and "thank you" goes a long way with the population. Think of how the other person might like to hear something phrased.

Make a Decision and Stick to it: Leaving your options open may be freeing for you, but it can make others nervous.

Find Other ORANGES: Some of the other colour styles may take offense to the "straight up" way you communicate and interpret a "harmless," playful comment as being "mean," "harsh," or "judgmental." Find other ORANGES so you can "let it all hang out." This will give you a channel for your energy and help prevent the wrong kinds of communication at inappropriate times.

ORANGES see themselves as:

Adaptable	Can deal with chaos	Capable	Carefree
Enjoying life	Flexible	Fun-Loving	Good negotiator
Hands-on	Multi-tasker	Practical	Proficient
Sees shades of gray	Spontaneous	Superior ability to distinguish among options	Welcomes new ideas

If I am a GREEN.

Being a GREEN, you are interested in facilitating smoother communication with others that do not embrace a similar style as yours. The following are techniques for further understanding their language and style.

Add some detail, or not: When asked to describe an experience, be aware of what the other person is requesting. Do they want just the big picture or some details? Some GREENS have a tendency to give only the big picture, while others may go into an in-depth explanation. Determine the appropriate strategy for relaying information according to the person you are communicating with.

Ease up: Notice whether your "why" questions are being misperceived as interrogation or as doubt of another person's intentions. If this is the case, use softeners to gain your answers, such as, "Please say more about ____ ."

Allow emotions: Just because others want to show their emotion does not mean that you are obligated to act or help them in any way. Let others express their feelings. Understand that's how some people process things.

Pay attention to other people's needs: Before charging ahead with your own agenda, take some time to gain understanding. A few minutes at the start of the conversation can save much time and frustration later for both of you. Notice the effect your behaviour has on others. Is your body language sending signals that you don't want to be approached?

Learn to listen without fixing: Many times people just want to be understood and heard - not every "problem" needs to be "fixed." Before the communication gets too far, politely ask them if they are seeking solutions or just a listening ear. This way you will know whether to listen for details or merely feelings. Simply listening and empathizing is a worthwhile activity in itself.

Acknowledge others' intent: Before offering correction, announce your understanding of the positive purpose behind others' behaviour. Skip the hurtful sarcasm or condescending tone. Instead, validate them with your feedback.

Save the debate: Although you may derive entertainment from playing "mental chess" with others, not everyone appreciates an intense discussion. Achieving a goal while alienating others can burn some bridges you may want to cross later.

Make time for your relationships: Notice what the people in your significant relationships need and appreciate. When feasible to do so, figure out what you can do to accommodate them - even if does not seem practical or logical.

Inform others: When you need to process, instead of just fading into your head to figure things out, let others know this is what you are doing. Notify them that you are not tuning them out, you simply would like some time to think. If you really want a challenge, allow others in on your processing. If your nature is to be introverted, change the experience by speaking your thoughts out loud, as they occur. Let others in on your analysis of the data.

GREENS see themselves as:

Able to find flaws	Precise, not repetitive	Able to reprimand	Powerful
Calm, not emotional	Rational	Creative	Eminently reasonable
Firm-minded	Objective	Seeking justice	Superior intellect
Under control	Visionary, original		

CHAPTER 8

HOW TO SELL TO?

When Selling to the ORANGE.

Now, when selling to the ORANGE there are a number of things to pay attention to. One, the ORANGE is spontaneous and will buy on impulse so the pre-packs and counter displays will be of interest to them. Be aware of the quick decisions that ORANGES make and be ready to give them quick sound bites of information, not a lot, just the immediate features and benefits. They may also be the one in the crowd or the line-up to shout, "excuse me " and seek out attention. They don't know that they are doing this however, it's just a part of their personality and they are naturally less inhibited than some of the other colours.

Two, the ORANGE will not always come to you with a 'specific' product in mind. They know that they are looking for something but they may not know exactly what that something is. For example, the ORANGE will ask for a foundation but they will not have a specific brand in mind. You will have to show this person 4 or 5 foundations and briefly explain what each one does. They will try each one on and look in the mirror to spot the minute differences between each and then they will ask to try "just one more" for comparison yet again. ORANGES love the demonstration part of the sale as they can become involved. They may actually take the product from your hand and decide to try it for themselves.

You may find the same to be true especially with fragrances. The ORANGE will come to you and ask for a fragrance with no idea what they are looking for in terms of the category. They may say something like, "I smelled something on someone yesterday and I want it" or "I need a new perfume…." Do not interpret the vagueness as ignorance per se. They enjoy the fun of the hunt. You will have to ask the following questions:

What type of fragrance are you looking for?
When do you want to wear it?
Is this for the office or for evening?
What are you wearing now?
Would you like something powerful or discrete? (probably not discrete)

Be ready to take some time with the ORANGE to help them determine what the correct choice is. You may also want to include samples of other fragrances as they are impulsive and may come back to purchase from the samples in addition to the sale you just made.

Another interesting characteristic of the ORANGE customer is that as you are showing them one product they will probably be looking at another. When shopping, the ORANGE is literally the proverbial kid in the candy store. They are not trying to be insulting to you as the sales associate - it's just the way they are.

Another characteristic of the ORANGE shopper is their unusual ability to bring others into the sale. They may solicit the opinions of strangers in the department without the slightest hesitation, as they are natural leaders who crave fun. Don't be at all surprised if the ORANGE customer asks the passerby for their opinion on the colour, cut or style of the item that you have shown them. They may change their choice two or three times as they are impulsive and do not dwell on past experiences or purchases but rather seek out the new and innovative and enjoy the accolades of others.

The ORANGE may also make choices that are less cautious than other individuals when it comes to colours. They make seek out bolder and more impactful shades for lips and eyes and can and will wear them with flair. Certainly, they will have nudes in the palette but they will be the ones coming to you to shop for reds and corals with confidence and will acknowledge the correct choice with glee! They are also more likely to have a collection of colours to wear with different outfits and will seek out colours to suit mood and situation.

All in all, the ORANGE is an enthusiastic consumer and will be fun to help through the sale. Just remember that the orange is a bright spot in the department while they are there and may just leave you with a couple of question marks in your head as well as a big smile on your face!

We will also add the challenges that can be faced, trying to sell to you palest colour.

When selling to the GOLD.

When selling to a GOLD it is important to remember a number of things. The GOLD is very practical which means that they will place a strong sense of need vs. want when purchasing a product. They will approach the need very seriously and arrive on your selling floor with a clear idea of what they intend to purchase. This client is clearly different than the ORANGE that you have dealt with earlier in the day. The ORANGE is fun oriented and likes to roam about the department without constraints. The GOLD will come to you with an empty package that they have saved to ensure that they go home with the exact, identical product as before or they may also come with a list to ensure that all needs are quite precisely met. If you, as the salesperson are dealing with a GOLD you may find that substitutions will not be tolerated. In other words, if the GOLD wants product X, then take them to that exact item without delay or deviation. It is of no consequence to the GOLD whatsoever that something may be updated or improved. You may find that they view this with skepticism and will voice that to you. They are not interested in trend items unless they have thoroughly reviewed the product on line or have tried it before and decided later that the item will be correct.

When the GOLD comes to you pay attention to what they are asking for and do not deviate from their requests. If they are seeking a particular product then provide that product without delay. You may, once the initial needs have been met, draw their attention to what is "new" or on trend but you will probably find that they have only a fleeting interest.

The most important thing to keep in mind with the GOLD customer is that they shop with an agenda. They wish to have their needs met with a minimum of fuss and do not want undue attention. You may also find that in some cases the GOLD does not solicit help at all and prefers to shop on their own. They do not necessarily dislike you as a salesperson and this is important to keep in mind so that you don't feel insulted when your offer to help is excused. It's just the way they are.

You may also find that the GOLD is the customer who is politically involved with the purchase that they are making and will seek out companies and manufacturers who are promoted as ethical and planet oriented as this will appeal to their sense of right and wrong. It can be of great concern to the GOLD that a product is of natural origin (also attractive to BLUE) or that the packaging is recycled or recyclable, or free of parabens, etc. When shopping this can be a make or break for the GOLD if indeed they are making a first time purchase so be sure to be able to talk to the research behind the item or the contributions that the manufacturer may make to the planet or health initiatives or sustainability. This is of importance to the GOLD and provides them with the feeling of inclusiveness, which they enjoy.

Also, if given the opportunity, the high GOLD may have the tendency to lean more in the direction of a product which is endorsed by someone with prestige. Like a well known, specialist in a field or a politically active celebrity.

When selling to the BLUE.

When it comes to selling, the BLUE may be one of the most challenging colors to sell to. It is not that the person themselves is challenging but rather that their modus operandi can be difficult to ascertain. Unlike an ORANGE who will be overt or the GOLD who will clearly identify their needs and wants the BLUE will be much more subtle when it comes to voicing their requirements.

As the BLUE is romantically motivated you may find that their purchases fit an established pattern that allows them to build on a situation. For example, the BLUE will purchase according to the season and the situation to create an ensemble that matches and can be coordinated with existing items in their wardrobe or home. In plain terms, they will "add to the pile" with a long-term goal in mind. This pattern could look something like this…. First, they may buy a navy sweater from you on the first encounter. The following week they may come back to you and purchase a blouse or shirt that corresponds to the sweater and then pick a piece of costume jewelry to go along with the existing sweater and the new top. The following week they may return to purchase shoes or a bag to go with the sweater, the top and the piece of costume jewelry. Rest assured that the BLUE has a definite idea in mind of what the completed ensemble will be and that look was the inspiration for the initial purchase. Each purchase for the BLUE will relate to the last one and they will establish that kind of buying pattern,

For the BLUE, one may say that correlation of purchases is of great importance. If one item is purchased randomly one may be assured that the next several purchases will be related to the previous one until the pattern is completed. It is as if the BLUE buys with an ultimate vision in mind to complete the self-created puzzle. It is not that the BLUE does not purchase randomly but rather that the seemingly random purchase will begin a series of future purchases until the desired effect is created. The process will take time but the BLUE consumer will return to you again and again until the desired effect is achieved as they start with the end in mind. One could say that patience could be a virtue when dealing with the BLUE and that is completely true but they are good and loyal customers who look to you as a resource both of material and understanding of their vision. That being said, if you are in a particularly busy environment and do not have a photographic memory it would be of value to keep a file of the previous purchases made by this customer so that you may refer back to previous encounters when new merchandise comes in. For example, when the new season of chocolate scarves arrives you could say to your BLUE customer, "I have just received some new and beautiful scarves in chocolates and caramels that would complement the camel merino wool suit that you purchased last season. I have 5 put aside just for you." Remember, the BLUE loves to be loved and feel that they are valued so this type of service will be greatly appreciated.

Another thing to bear in mind when selling to the BLUE is that feelings and emotion will also play a role in purchasing and the "experience" of the sale is of great importance. They like acknowledgement and enjoy a friendly and cozy environment when shopping. Learn the name of the BLUE client and use it during the sale. BLUES do not like feeling anonymous when they are purchasing and wish to see that you remember the last time they dealt with you so make sure to talk to the last purchase and inquire as to how the item has been integrated into their wardrobe or home. You will make big points with this customer by doing this.

It is important to remember with the BLUE customer that the relationship with you is as important as the merchandise that you are showing or selling. YOU are the person that they deal with and you will be that person going forward as they are all about the feeling of belonging to something. BLUES enjoy the familiarity of one-on-one relations with all of their service providers and this applies as much to you in retail as it does to their dealing with their florist, insurance agent, car dealership, or butcher. They want YOU to help them and will wait for your personal attention.

It is wise not to hand your BLUE customer to a co-worker if you are busy and they arrive at your place of business unannounced. They will take this as a personal slight. After all, in the BLUE'S mind, the visit with you during the sale is almost as important as the item they came for. Take this as an extreme compliment from the BLUE. If you are with another client take the time to tell your BLUE that you will be with them in a moment. Offer them a seat if you are able and a refreshment if at all possible. They will wait for you but not too, too long. BLUES are some of the best and most consistent customers that you will ever have and they will share you with their friends and family. It is not at all unusual for the BLUE to send you referrals once they have established a relationship with you. Many days you may have a new person in front of you saying "I'm a friend of X and she told me that you were the person to talk to about……"

Something to read between the lines here is that you will never get away with bad service when dealing with a BLUE. They would much rather that you be honest and say "no" to the fit or the color or the cut than say "yes" in order to make the sale. You will find that the BLUE will not be unhappy so much with the garment as with the salesperson as they expect total integrity from you. You can bet your life that if you lack integrity in selling to the BLUE that the item may be returned but the BLUE will not.

So get your client book open!

When selling to the GREEN.

This colour might be one of the most challenging for you to sell to depending on the commodity that you are selling. Certainly, you will find that your technical knowledge will be not only needed greatly but will be put to the test in terms of accuracy. Also, you will find that emotion is not really a key factor in the purchase. This customer is all about logic and purpose and the intent of the purchase is to fulfill a very distinct intellectual need. You will not find this customer in the 'spontaneity' section of your store.

Let's just put it out on the table. The GREEN is controlled and careful in their purchase patterns and will probably have done prior research before they will come to seek your assistance. Be ready for this client and be fully knowledgeable with your facts and figures when dealing with them or you may have a slightly unpleasant experience on your hands. They do not take well to answers that are even remotely ambiguous.... give the GREEN the straight goods or you will not have a happy customer.

If you are an opposing color such as ORANGE you may even wish to rehearse and role-play your selling style when you are confronted with a GREEN. You may be impulsive and full of excitement about the product or service that you are selling but this is not what appeals to your GREEN customer. They are simply not interested in hype or superfluous details. For example, if you were selling a car to a GREEN you will find that when they come to your showroom they have already done their research on the vehicle. It is the engine and that mileage that will appeal to the GREEN. Likewise, they will be interested in the options that are available but it will not be for the prestige of the options but rather how they will enhance the value of the car and improve the driving experience from A to B. They may be concerned about the paint but it won't be about the color but rather about the warranty, quality and number of coats. Put it this way, an ORANGE will be enthused by the finish of the vehicle. The GREEN will want to know what it took to get it that way and how long it will stay there.

Another characteristic of the GREEN in the selling world is that they will not solicit your help initially. As I have stated earlier, before they have come to your place of business they have researched the product and carefully considered how it will impact their lives. They will have done comparative pricing, checked out the situation on-line, inquired into reviews, and may be making their second trip into your shop. Be ready and willing to share with the GREEN all that you may have in terms of reading material, stats, service concerns and issues, warranty and guarantee variables, safety ratings, consumer reviews and the like. This is what they are after as well as the product.

You may even find it beneficial to include a work associate who has a greater knowledge of the product than you do. Your GREEN customer will appreciate the extra time and effort that you have put into servicing them. If you are unsure of your footing with your product this will be of great advantage in closing the sale.

It is not that the GREEN seeks to "out-tech" or "out –intellectualize" you but rather that the perfectionist in them will present itself to you when they come to purchase. They want answers and will ask the questions needed to get those answers so be ready and on your game.

CHAPTER 9

WE HAVE ALL COLOURS

Blend of Colours - we have all four colours, what triggers what? We have spent some time discussing the brightest and palest of your colours, the one thing we still need to go over is the one thing we seem to overlook. *We have all four colours.*

Many people have the majority of their individuality in one colour, and rarely seek the characteristics of their other colours. My question to you is this, 'Why is it important to understand colour spectrums'? It is critical for many reasons. The first is that we are all a full colour spectrum, we have all four colours in us.

However, we do have a blend of different variations, 24 to be exact, whether we use them or not. The colours other than our brightest colour can and do influence our behaviours. Choosing to refer to ourselves as one colour type is neither accurate nor precise.

For example, if I were to refer to myself as "I'm an Orange" it would not be a precise statement. My brightest of colours is ORANGE, however, I do have all other colours within my spectrum. This gives me the ability to reach in and utilize these skills when required.

Your colour combination is factored on your first and second colour. The influence and power of the second colour provides an insight to the whole person.

A common thought pattern is that many people find that their first and second colours are equally strong and interchangeable. They are so closely tangled that they merge together. At certain times you will be confused which of the two colours is dominant. For some individuals, their second color does influence their first in a very strong way and for others it may have a minimal effect.

Popular Blends
Challenging Blends

There are colour blends that may be contrary to each other. For example, BLUES make decisions based on how they feel and/or the impact those decisions may have on others vs. the GREEN who's decisions are all based on facts and logic. In addition, ORANGES seem to get the most out of life when pushing the boundaries and being spontaneous when the GOLDS like to enforce the rules and be organized.

Now, how can they both be dominant within one person? Aren't these blends of colours not a direct conflict with each other? You would think so. Let's take a look at these colour blends.

BLUE - GREEN.

What an interesting blend this is. The individual with BLUE-GREEN is particular. With the BLUE the primary or equal to GREEN, they will put feelings and nurturing in the forefront. The GREEN with its logical perspective will show itself to try and control emotions. They may presume what others want and will adjust themselves accordingly to them. Most of the time they are caring, and considerate of others. The GREEN will also have a strong urge to hold back, not show too much emotion, and will have a tendency to be alone with their thoughts. They will get frustrated if the work is not perfect, and will relate to systems rather than people when at work. Keep in mind that the GREEN considers work as play.

GREEN - BLUE.

Even though you may think that the BLUE - GREEN would be very similar in personality traits, there are some distinct differences. The blend of GREEN being the primary and BLUE secondary comes at a cost of being mostly misunderstood. They work at a global level of thinking, setting a standard for themselves that is quite high. They may choose to avoid certain public functions, social events or even family gatherings. Their preference would be to stay home and read, and/or go on a fact-finding mission.

The BLUE will take it very personally when people do not respond and choose not to socialize, send messages, e-mails or voice mail. This side of them will be hurt and will push the GREEN to isolate even further. If you say something that will hurt them, unfortunately the GREEN will cover up all emotions and leave no traces of an emotional wound. The GREEN - BLUE may feel they are open-minded and communicative, and want people to like and understand them without having to go into personal explanations.

Remember that the GREEN/BLUE – BLUE/GREEN have the ability to see opportunities or possibilities where most people cannot. The have a great ability to see the global aspect of things.

ORANGE – GOLD.

Hold on! The ORANGE-GOLD blend is a fun loving person who wants to get things moving, "When would **Now** be a good time." Today is when things happen, tomorrow is only a mystery. They move forward at the risk of not assessing the hazards ahead. This is where the GOLD comes into play, providing the planning and guidance. The GOLD can leave them feeling regret and guilt for moving so fast, so they live in a world of "rather ask for forgiveness than permission," but will review the consequences when things settle down. Nobody needs to beat them down as they do a fine job on their own. When planning ahead and getting things organized, you allow them the freedom they need to thrive and shine. You love their company simply because they are ready to take on any challenge placed in front of them, they motivate and create new ways of living life to its fullest.

GOLD- ORANGE.

The GOLD-ORANGE has quite a different challenge than the ORANGE-GOLD as their drive is responsibility at all cost. No fun can be had unless all is done properly and correctly, if unprepared they will turn you back to do it properly. The ORANGE will want to be spontaneous, however, the

GOLD will hold them back. They will pull themselves away from social events, simply due to responsibilities or commitments. You would be fascinated by the internal dialogue that goes on within themselves in regards to what is the right or wrong thing to do.

Both the GOLD-ORANGE and ORANGE-GOLD blends can be a commanding association. Their self-confidence, practicality, take charge, plan ahead, dependable and consistent traits make them remarkable people.

Opposites Working Together

We see these blends as being self-conflicts, internal turmoil's on a consistent basis, but the truth is that they create an alliance, a synergy of characteristics that allow these individuals the ability to create and move things forward with more accuracy, speed, perfection and love than anyone you know. Your task is to channel this energy in their natural tendencies.

GOLD - GREEN

The GOLD - GREEN blend, is a strong combination of facts, details and data, never coming to a decision that has not been thoroughly thought through. These individuals bring forward results that have amazing views, structure, planning and details. They can also get lost in their work, leaving the world behind. They do not reach the emotional levels others around them may require, as understanding and feelings are certainly alien to them.

GOLD - BLUE

The GOLD - BLUE has a fabulous capacity to comprehend what needs to be done, what the processes are and how to bring the group together under one idea. The GOLD personality sees a traditional way to move forward or provides the right answer. The BLUE personality blends in the insights about the people involved and how they can be an asset.

GREEN - ORANGE

The blend of GREEN-ORANGE is a highly active individual, wonderful with ideas and action. They see solutions and/or possibilities and take action quickly. The incredible strength these people have is without a doubt to catch sight of an idea and before anyone else has had the ability to process it they have taken action. You must also understand that this behaviour will make many others uneasy and intolerant of such quick action. The GREEN-ORANGE is impatient and moves without thought of others. They live in the '**Ready - Fire - Aim**' world of doing things.

GREEN - GOLD

The GREEN-GOLD has a distinct way of working. First idea, then plan (always). They are the thinkers who see the big picture from start to finish in their minds, then translate this information to the teams so to achieve the desired outcome. We often see this type of person in the C-suites (CEO, COO, CFO, etc.) or other executive type positions. They must however be aware of their inability to be attached on an emotional level. You can say that they may not see the trees from the forest when it comes to personal interaction.

ORANGE - BLUE

Here stands the individual who reaches out to others. ORANGE has the drive, "No Fear / I have nothing to lose" type of attitude when it comes to meeting others. Their positive nature is attractive to others and creates an compelling force. When combined with the BLUE'S social ability and "people person" attributes, they can easily make quick connections with others.

ORANGE - GREEN

In front of you is a person that has the ability to create and is open to possibilities. The ORANGE is the one that is in the driver's seat while the

GREEN keeps the thinking process in motion. Each of these colours are innovators, creators and can see potential in all things. Living in the world of "Just do it" and "Why not?" makes them leaders in the world of change.

BLUE - ORANGE

The BLUE-ORANGE are the people persons, living for the joy of connecting with others. Their positive nature and joy for life makes them easy to connect with. Befriending these people is easy, you want to be near them. You will find them working for others and making the world around them a much better place. Their ORANGE will push them to meet and enjoy others.

BLUE - GOLD

Our BLUE-GOLD is the person whose allegiance to others in unquestionable. They are motivated by their connections with others, the willingness to truly know them and shared with the GOLD their loyalty is "Through thick and thin, I will stand by you." They can be overly tolerant of negative situations and will be hoping that things change much longer than anyone else.

Same Colour Blend - Different People

When you meet someone with the same color blend as yourself you will immediately make a connection. You may feel as if they are a long lost friend and you will be able to have a meaningful discussion in regards to their needs and what they may be looking for. This customer will want to build a relationship with you and you with them.

CHAPTER 10

OUR STORIES

GREEN Coffee

Monday through Friday Alice handles the front counter at a coffee shop. She starts her day at about 5:30 a.m. when she rushes to the store to get ready for a 6:00 a.m. opening. While many are still sleeping Alice rushes about to get ready to meet and greet her ever-growing crowd of customers.

Alice knows her regulars and greets each one by name if she can remember and if she can't recall the customers' names she knows their order off by heart. She wants to start their morning with a smile and a cup of their favourite beverage piping hot and fresh. Her customers come to her specifically and will wait for her service, which she wants to be the best.

6:10 a.m. and Tony comes bounding through the door in his usual rush to get to the gym before he goes to his office. "Morning Alice!! The usual please!" he says as she pours a large black coffee into the paper cup. "Morning Tony! Here ya go" she says and passes the much needed liquid into his hands. "Thanks Alice! See you tomorrow." Tony says and he heads out the door.

Next comes Sylvia, with her usual order of a double espresso that she will enjoy at the table in the corner by the window like she does every day as she checks her e-mails. Jane comes next for a 'no fat' milk cappuccino that she has on Monday only as her treat for the week. Jane is dieting this week the same as last week and every other week before and Alice makes sure to ask her how the diet is going like she does every Monday. Jane beams and tells Alice that she is down a pound. "Hooray for you Jane! It must be the no fat milk!" If you haven't guessed, Alice's primary colour is GOLD and making her customers happy is very important to her.

Charlie comes in next, then Nadia, then Gary and Ravshan and Olga. Alice knows them all and is ready for them. Perfect coffees, clean cups and the dull roar of morning conversations and newspapers rustling. Alice looks up from the espresso machine and tells herself that it's going to be a good day in the neighbourhood. Just then, Harold (A high GREEN) comes in. "Oh no!" thinks Alice. In her head she remembers the first time that Harold came in last week and the hoops he put her through. The questions!! The questions!!

"How fresh are the beans?

" Is this coffee a certain temperature?"

"Do you have 2% milk?"

"How long has this pot been on the heat?"

"Do you use filtered water or tap?"

Alice summons her courage and goes into her mental files from her first encounter with Harold the high GREEN. "Good Morning Harold" she says "I'm just putting on a fresh pot of coffee for you made with the filtered water that we use for all our customers and I have just ground the beans fresh as you can see." Harold looks at Alice and nods approval as the fresh dark liquid pours into the waiting pot.

"Harold, I know you like your coffee a certain temperature so I will put the thermometer in the coffee for you to see that its right and I have a choice of sugar for you. There's brown, white and rock sugar for you today on the station to your left and the milk was just opened 2 minutes before you came in."

Alice finishes pouring the coffee for Harold and passes the cup to him across the counter. "I hope you will enjoy your coffee!" she says, as Harold looks at her somewhat perplexed.

Harold pays for the coffee and goes to the station with the milk and sugars to adjust the coffee to his particular taste. He sips the coffee as he passes towards a table in the far back of the café away from others. Solitary, he finishes the coffee and sits in contemplation. After a few minutes Harold gets up and goes to the counter again. Alice, seeing this gets ready for what she thinks is another question about her skills…ugh.

Instead, Harold says to her "Alice, its Alice correct? I would just like to say thank you for a wonderful cup of coffee and your great service this morning. It's not often that I get coffee the way that I think it should be and you did it. I just opened my office 3 doors down and I have 20 people working for me. You will supply coffee to all our meetings and I will send my clients to you but you must make the coffee just the way you did this morning. OK?"

"I would be happy to provide you with coffee just like this morning Harold." Alice says with a smile "but I did not get your last name…." "GREEN," declares Harold "my name is Harold Green of Green and Co, Coffee International."

Alice breathed in slightly, smiled and said " See you tomorrow Mr. Green?"

"You can count on that, 6:25 a.m. precisely and you can call me Harold."

Apples to Apples, ORANGES to ORANGES

"Good morning Tom, how was the weekend, any wind surfing or bike racing? The apple orchard is open for business. I bought a bushel of them and I have apples for everyone today, want one?" said the train porter to one of the regular commuters on the train service to the city. A daily commute of 45 minutes to downtown, which would normally take a little under two hours by car. The train commute provides comfortable seating, tables and plug-in's for your cell phone and laptops, space to walk around and soft music to make the trip a comfortable one.

Our train conductor Dan, is a happy go lucky type of individual, he see's each day as a new opportunity to meet and greet people, very aware of who is who and making the best out of everything. Smiles are free in Dan's world.

Tom is a very active person and owner of a sports shop in the downtown core, never spends anytime floundering or dithering about. Dan, like Tom, can relate to each other by the activities they do. It's always fabulous for Dan to hear how Tom spends his weekends and Dan never misses an opportunity to simply sit and chat.

Tom kept walking to the nearest of seats, not his usual seat next to the exit so to be first one out, making a game out of every moment. Today was a very different day for Tom, he was held back, withdrawn and very, very quiet. Most days, Tom cannot stop talking about his weekend adventures, as an avid sportsmen he also will be the first to try something new, his latest adventure was wind surfing. With no big water in his area, he had always wanted to try surfing, but with that not being available, he did the next best thing. Dan rejoiced when Tom had explained to him what he had tried and enjoyed, explained his challenges with staying on the board, the flips, tumbles and turns that had been all parts of the learning curves.

Nothing was said, just a quiet walk to his seat. Immediately Dan knew there was something wrong, something that had caused Tom to withdraw from everything and everyone. He slowly followed Dan to his seat and kept walking to the next car.

You can say that Dan had this wonderful ability to know when to push for information and when not to. He went about his business, ensuring that all passengers were comfortable.

On his way back to Tom's seat, Dan had gone to the dining car and picked up a medium size coffee, double, double. He knew that was how Tom liked his coffee. He stopped in front of Tom's table and said "Not sure how things are going with you my friend, but I thought you may need this," and put down the coffee on the table. Still no word, Tom was lost in his own thoughts and Dan did not notice that Tom was looking outside.

Fifteen minutes had gone by when Dan decided to do his rounds again, stopping and asking if everything was fine with everyone and to let them know just how much time was left before their destination. As he crossed from one car to another, he opened the door and felt the surge of wind, meaning only one thing, the door was open.

Let me also tell you this, Dan is not only a great porter, but is also partially blind. Dan was a very active individual in his days, would bike every day, swim when he could and had the chance to do some skydiving. Never has anyone heard him say 'Those were the days'. His challenge is to see the world in a whole different way, not feeling sorry for himself or for what someone had done but to embrace life to its fullest. Dan was a victim of a drunk driver. He was doing his daily biking when the driver had fallen asleep at the wheel and his car drove on to the shoulder where Dan was biking. It was a tragic accident, however, with his will to live and passion for life in two short years he had made an exceptional recovery. The only issues that remained were the scars and Dan being partially blind. These were obstacles he was able to deal with and had returned to work so to be with the people he so much enjoyed.

Dan stopped between the cars and moved slowly to the door, which swung inward, meaning if he got himself in the wrong position and the door would swing back shut, he would be thrown off the train. As he moved he felt a person on the floor, "Excuse me, but this is not the place to be", Dan said with a very calm voice.

Dan could see the shape of a person sitting on the floor, but could not say who it was. No matter what the situation, Dan had a great ability to take charge, no panic, just 'Let's get it under control'. He knelt down to be closer, put his hand on the persons side and said "Are you OK?".

"No, I just want to be alone". Dan quickly realized that the voice he had just heard was Tom's. Dan may be visually impaired, however, voices stayed permanently imprinted in his mind.

"What's up my friend?" Dan asked without trying to show too much concern or worry

Tom waited a few seconds and replied, "I just want to left alone Dan, it's not a good day and I'd much rather not share this with anyone." The one thing you notice of in a person who is a high ORANGE, is that they will isolate themselves when things are going very wrong, not wanting the world to see their sorrow.

Dan was well aware of this and he knew it had to be severe for Tom to be out here, "Tom, are we friends?" Dan asked with a clear voice.

Tom asked without hesitation, "You know we are, what kind of question is that?"

"It's a question one friend would ask another, so my friend, what brings you out here between the cars with the door opened? I'm freezing here." Dan said in as much of a happy voice as he possibly could.

"Oh! Dan, if I don't answer you, you'll stay here for the whole damn ride, won't you?" Tom said keeping his head down.

Dan felt he was making some headway, "You know it, once a pain in the ass, always a pain. Tools of who we are." He was proud and on a roll, he didn't want to let Tom think anymore. He knew he had to get him talking. "Remember when I got in my accident, after two years I came back and really didn't want to be on this train. I felt I couldn't do the job properly, that it would be best if they gave the job to someone else. What did you say to me that very first day you saw me back? I think you were the only one who recognized me."

Tom answered, smiling slightly "Who could forget a person with a mug like yours, always smiling and happy. You could have asked the doctors to do a little plastic surgery on your face to add a few years on, is what I said," Tom answered.

Dan did not miss a heartbeat, he wanted to engage Tom in a discussion of who they were, so he kept on "Most of the passengers were trying to move out of the way to let me go by, even had a few idiots passing their hands in front of my face. You on the other hand, just talked about how 'pretty' I was and laughed. Not in an insulting or rude way, but in a fashion that only I could understand. You took the time for me, you didn't feel sorry for me, you just wanted me to get up and smell the coffee and stop feeling sorry for myself. You had the courage to address that head-on with me and I appreciated that."

Dan didn't notice but Tom was looking right at him, Dan had Tom engaged and he was not going to let go, "We, my friend, are not the type of people to give up. Yes, we get a kick in the wazoo once and a while but we still move forward! I would assume you received a hell of a kick to be in this frame of mind. But I'm glad you're sorry butt is on my train today, if anyone can get you off the floor, it would be me."

When you have great similarities with someone, you can almost feel what they are feeling and that is a gift of the high ORANGE's, insight. Believe me they know how to use it.

Dan let out a little laugh, "I must look like a real loser, don't I?"

"No my friend, you look like Tom, a great man with a gift to offer the world. But you can't do that sitting here between the cars, let's go have a coffee" Dan put his hand in Tom's direction.

Tom reached and grabbed his hand, "Ok, let's go finish that coffee some sensitive sap left on my table, I bet it was cold to start off with." He said laughing out loud. Dan turned and shut the door. "Thank you Tom, I wish you could know just how good it feels to have someone like you around, you're a good man and I am grateful. Just so you know, and I don't want to spend to much time on this, I think I have felt sorry for myself long enough and it's time to get up and moving, my wife left me last night, said I didn't spend enough time at home with her." Tom paused for a moment, taking a breath of courage to tell his story, "She likes to stay home, same routine over and over, she's a wonderful woman and great mother to our son, but has a hard time with me not 'relaxing' like she wants. I've tried to get her involved in the business, go kayaking, biking, hiking and all sorts of sports but she wants to stay home with me by her side. I can't, and it's when I got a seat for our son on my bike, she lost it!" He threw his hands in the air, "I had the best of all the equipment for the little guy, as safe as it can be. No way! she said, you will not make him a crazy kid like you. I have enough with one in the family and I can see it in him already, you're crazy influence." He became silent again.

"Last night, when I got home, there was a note on the table, she had left, gone to her parents where life is more structured and organized for her and our son. It took the wind out of my sails, I felt like a kid in school again, could not do anything write, always doing what I wanted and now it is happening all over again. I must admit, I wanted to end it all, I could not go through this again. You can say that I had a moment of weakness and it sucks." Dan felt Tom's pain. Dan continued, "He's my son, he is full of life, full of energy and I don't want him to live under the expectations of others. I want him to be himself, to get up early in the morning and appreciate the sun rise and go for a run or ride or what ever he wants to do. I want him to go fast if he wants, to take the risks in life. I did, I started my little business as a bicycle repair shop and today it's a sports shop in downtown valued at 6 million dollars. I'd say it's a risk that paid off, but I failed a number of times."

Tom was pouring it out. He had his confidence back, he just needed to open the gates and let it out, "That's what I wanted for my family. She told me she loved me that way and now it's all changed. It was fun at first to sit and watch a movie but I can't do that every single day. Now she wants that for our son and I couldn't have that. On the bike when he came with me, he was in his glory, all he was saying was 'Go Daddy Go', and we had fun."

"Thank you for pulling me out of the depths of self pity my friend, I did feel like I was a child in prison, being told I was inadequate as a father. My soul was sinking and I was losing what was part of me, my son." Leaning against the train car he stopped for a moment in reflection. "I know I can't give up, I know I need to be there for my son and he needs his Dad, again, thank you Dan."

Tom put his hand on Dan's shoulder and started walking towards his table. "I think I will take the day off Dan" Tom said.

"Why's that?" Dan replied.

"I just got a new double-seated racing bike that I was going to use for my wife and I and pull our son in a little trailer behind, it's made of the top end alloy.It's a spectacular piece of engineering and so, since my wife doesn't want to come for a ride maybe my friend who gets off work at the next stop might be interested in coming for a ride and trying it out with me, so what do you say, want to try it out Dan? By the way, I'll have one of your apples also, if you're still giving them away." Tom was back to be himself again.

Dan was thrilled to hear Tom's voice back to its happy self. "Only if I can be in front, we need to work on your vocal cords, and have you scream-ing like a little boy when we fly through the traffic from lane to lane with you in back wearing a sign that says **Blind Guy Driving**!" They both burst out laughing and sat down to continue their great discussion until the train arrived.

A high ORANGE will know how to reach another high ORANGE. Not by using sympathy but by using a clear and direct message to bring what is important to an ORANGE - 'Fun'. Tom and Dan were able to con-nect at a their own level, supporting one another in a moment of need with the use of humour, making life fun again.

Why change

Heather manages a very high-end boutique in downtown Boston. The store has a well-established reputation for quality, excellence, class and superior service. The boutique has been in operation for over 25 years, and was started by Heather's father, Karl. The store had taken birth out of Karl's enthusiasm and passion to make a difference in Boston's fashion community. When Karl started the boutique he was faced with all sorts of criticisms, challenges, rudeness and ridicule from his own family. Karl persisted and created a world-class shop in the downtown core of Boston despite his family and the naysayers. Karl had been perceived as a dreamer, as one who took unrealistic risks and putting his family in harm's way. His wife, Bonnie, on the other hand, believed in him so much she worked two jobs to ensure that the children did not go without and he could follow his dreams.

The boutique first started out very small. Karl's vision was to support local designers and promote their garments in a world-class fashion. Even though the shop was small, the presentation of the garments was spectacular. The pieces were displayed wonderfully, with a carefully selected background to enhance each item and to bring them to life. The window was changed weekly to give variety and provide an opportunity to all designers that shared his vision, passion and commitment to fashion. Karl would also support the designers by hosting fashion shows on the street, weather permitting. Karl understood marketing and sales, quality and great customer service.

Karl's dream was to keep his 'Vision' of promoting local designers, and it worked. After a number of years, the boutique's reputation grew, sales increased and it attracted the attention of many big chain stores.

He had been approached by a number of big brand name stores to sell his boutique or to partner. The offers were to move his boutique in their stores and to carry out his plan on a bigger scale. Even though the idea was tempting, his research showed that many store owners that had made such a move had all been pushed aside, and the designers were taken from them, leaving the store owner with little to nothing to call their own. Karl stood his ground and maintained his authenticity.

His motivation was not purely financial, it was his passion for the variety of world-class designs he provided his customers and he loved his ability to demonstrate the quality, originality in the window displays. People would gather together to look and discuss the new fashions every week. It was the cutting edge of fashion and Karl was the creator.

Despite the challenges of starting up a new business, Karl and his wife Bonnie had four children to care for. He and Bonnie believed in letting their children decide on their own what they wanted to do with their lives and encouraged them to be authentic. Karl, like many parents would not force his children to do things. He and Bonnie believed in encouraging their children to be creative and inventive, but despite all the encouragement they all chose the safe route in life.

The two boys followed the path of their grandfather, working at the refinery just out of town, the eldest of his daughters chose to be a nurse for the simple security of a job at the hospital and Heather the youngest, chose the accounting world.

Karl and Bonnie were free spirits. They believed in making a difference, however, both of their parents were very conservative, not wanting to 'rock the boat' type of thing. Karl's father once told him, "Why do you need to be so different, why do you have to stand out. Why can't you be like everyone else, get a good job, consistent pay and good security? No! You need to make waves, let everyone know you're here." Karl never answered his father, he knew it would be pointless. Instead of discouraging Karl, it motivated him to move forward, to make a difference and to show the family that he could do it, he could be successful. He was successful but that didn't matter. The comments continued 'It will not last, You're just being lucky'. You would think that with all the success Karl and Bonnie were having, that the consistent family badgering would stop, that they would see that his idea worked, but it didn't.

After 20 years the boutique had become very successful, Karl and Bonnie were being recognized by Boston's Chamber of Commerce and the Mayor for their great service and fabulous commitment to the city's downtown core. With the award came a wonderful gift. They were presented with an all-expense paid trip to France and tickets to attend one of the world's greatest fashion shows, with a backstage pass and post fashion show party to see where all the business is done. The opportunity of a life time.

This trip and fashion show was one of Karl's biggest dreams. In order to start the boutique his family had sacrificed so much, for so long, that this dream had been put aside. He never imagined that he would ever be able to attend such a show. Now it was here and it was being given to him and his wife for their hard work and persistence.

Sadly, the only member of the family that attended the Boston event was Heather, sitting, listening to the people talking about her mother and father's success. She was very proud of them, but it pained her that she had put so little interest in the business. Here she was, sitting with a few thousand people who had come recognize the hard work her parents had done. Strangers were coming up to her and congratulating her for her parent's success, saying how she should be so proud of their accomplishments for the past 20 years. Heather, was only 19 years of age and two years of University behind her, and was unclear as to what she had missed out on. One thing she did know was that she needed to do a lot of catching up with her parents.

On their way home, Heather sat in the back of the car in silence, listening to her parents chat about this and that person, and how their little boutique had changed their life. How many different designers they had supported over the years, how they had the opportunity to show the community and the world what they could do. Finally Heather spoke, "Ok, what was that all about, I feel like you two are complete strangers. My parents are nothing like the two people who everyone was talking about, my parents are not the ones who get recognized by thousands as people who are making a difference in the world. Who are you two?"

Karl and Bonnie laughed out loud, "Heather, this is the work we have been doing. It has been a challenge and many sacrifices had to be made, and most importantly, we didn't want to burden you kids with what we were going through." Karl paused for a moment and then continued, "You know that we had no support and were actually encouraged to close the boutique. Your mother worked two jobs for a number of years so that we could survive financially and I sometimes took a night job to bring extra money, but we persisted. Today, we are privileged to have you come and join us in the most gratifying event of our lives, we watched as people came to shake your hands. We knew you weren't aware and that you would have many, many questions, so let's get started", Karl said with a smile.

Heather looked at her father and then her mother, "Where was I in all this, Why didn't I see any of this?"

"Not one of you ever did, you stayed with your grandparents on weekends when we had a lot of work, to their displeasure I must add." Bonnie said as she turned in her seat. "You see, the family wanted us to do what everyone else was doing, however that would have killed your father and I love him too much to see him in a job that gave him no satisfaction. He is my hero. I loved him then and still love him. He never gave up on his dream" she was touching his shoulder as he was driving.

Heather had a moment of recollection, remembering her grandparents remarks, "So that is why we heard all those sarcastic comments from our grandparents," Heather said. "Yes!" answered Karl.

Bonnie continued, "You see Heather, we are all so very different, we all see life a different way. Your father is free as an eagle, he could never be held in one place. Look, he can't even follow the speed limits!" she burst out laughing and so did Karl as he looked at the speedometer.

Heather looked at her mother and asked, "What about you mom, how do you fit in to all of this?"

Bonnie smiled with so much love in her heart, "I fell in love with a man who had a dream, he had spirit and wanted to not only be a success but he wanted to help the people of his community. He was an honorable man, even though others didn't see him that way. Just don't give him a cheque book, he could not balance that if his life depended on it," she said with a short laugh.

Bonnie looked at Heather and said, "What we found interesting is that all our four children love the status quo. You don't like change, you are very comfortable with a consistent routine. Believe me, that is a great pleasure to us, however, you do notice that others have a different way of being. No one person is better than the other, it's all how they see the world and do things." She paused for a moment and then continued, "We have noticed this in so many people, the different way they act, talk and listen. Take a bit of time, and look how your father adjusts his presentation to each and every customer that comes in the store. If he needs to add detail he does. Some people are in and out. Some only want to talk. Some people call for appointments. That's all OK, he makes adjustment."

"Not everyone is the same and we know that. We didn't learn that in a day, it took time, patience and many, many failures. But we got back up, we kept going and tried again." She was looking directly at Heather who was in full attention to what her mother was saying.

Heather was in awe. She was amazed at what her mother was saying. Heather was very curious as to see how her parents analyzed so many people, figured out a way to relate to what their needs were, and build a relationship with them. She understood very well the importance of not just '**Good**' service, but providing '**Great**' service. Heather had witnessed that evening what great work her parents had done to achieve these results. She felt ashamed not having known or wanting to know or showing any interest in their lives. Life was "Ok" and that had been good enough for her and her siblings.

Having had a glimpse of just how much work and understanding of their customers her parents had done, Heather was thinking; 'people noticed what I took for granted'.

A series of emotions were flowing through her. Karl looked back in the rear view mirror and noticed the look on his youngest daughter's face,

"What are you thinking about Heather? What's going on in that wonderful mind of yours? Want to share?" Shaking her head Heather replied, "No Dad, I'm just reliving the evening and my life really." She continued, "I can't believe I have had my head in the sand for so long. How my sister and brothers talked about the insignificance of the store. When we would go to our grandparent's homes, they would say 'If they worked a normal job, you kids would not have to be here, you could be with your parents where you belong. Your father and his crazy dreams'. We never understood the comments, we were young and only wanted to have fun."

Karl interrupted, "Heather, it wasn't your responsibility to understand. Your only responsibility was to dream and to create things in your mind. We wanted you to be free in society. Fortunately, not everyone sees life the same, we need people who like consistency, the status quo and a good sense of structure. They, like you, keep things in a consistent state of regularity to help keep people like me in line. Even though I do not enjoy the suggestion of certain things, depending on the approach, I can consider it." With a smile he looked at the speedometer to see how fast he was going and Bonnie let out a little chuckle.

For the rest of the drive home, Heather was in her own head, reliving over and over the evening, the comments, the praises given by strangers about how wonderful her parents were and how hard they had worked to achieve such a success.

Karl and Bonnie did not have a lot of time to plan for their trip, but that was no worry. Karl loved the last minute rush. Heather was going to be off on study week and Karl asked if she would not mind working at the store while they were in Paris. Not having spent much time in the store and never actually having worked there, she was nervous. Bonnie had Heather spend a day with her in the store before they left. She showed her the daily routines, payments, staff guide lines and any expected deliveries scheduled for the week. Heather was very comfortable with this, but it was the customers she was unsure of. Bonnie assured her that it was going to be OK! "Just be yourself, don't try and work like your father or I, people see through someone who is not authentic."

During the week that Karl and Bonnie were gone so many things happened that caused Heather to gain more clarity on life and what customer service was all about. The changes came very quickly.

72

The first experience was Monday afternoon. The media announced a massive lay-off at the refinery where her two brothers were working. Customers were coming in to the store asking to talk with Karl and Bonnie. It seemed like they had a way with people. Customers just came in and asked 'Where is Karl or Bonnie, I need their advice'. At first she let them know that they would be absent for the week, but she noticed the look of desperation on their faces and wanted to help.

"Can I be of any help?" Heather asked a gentleman that was just standing there, looking lost. "You see young lady, your father was and is an inspiration for me. He always encouraged me to think outside the box and your mother is a loving soul. I was thinking about starting my own business and your parents shared the struggles they had on their journey. I am a creature of habit and I know that, but I always felt that security in a job was only an imaginary thing. Karl had said once, 'You create your own security', and I've never forgotten that. Now the refinery is letting me go and I'm not sure what to do." The gentlemen said with worry on his face. Heather thought for a moment and replied, "I may not be the best at this, but I did listen to my parents and I have spent too much time doing 'what was expected of me' by everyone. You see Sir, only recently have I learned how wonderful my parents are and the hard work they did to provide for us and let us live our own life, even if it was the 'safe' life. May I suggest something, if that's OK with you?" The gentlemen made a slight nod of the head. She continued "If starting your business is a dream, I recommend you live it to the fullest, and your customers will see just how much you care and doing business with you will brighten their day and improve your business." Heather looked at him for his response. "Young lady, as my parents would have said, 'the apple does not fall far from the tree', and you are living proof of that. Thank you." He shook her hand and walked out with a little jump in his step.

Heather was operating the boutique with accuracy and precision, very proud to be assisting the clients and customers who came to the store in their particular needs. The process was as we may say 'a natural fit' for Heather, great customer service was what she could truly relate to.

Now what was going on with the community and her brothers was a little different, the lay off at the refinery was causing havoc, fear had settled in and those who were seeking security were lost. Heather's brothers were part of that group, blaming the corporate office for lack of compassion and only thinking of the bottom line and not of the people. Only a few days had gone by since the media release and all hell broken loose.

Karl and Bonnie were scheduled to be back home early on Sunday morning, taking the redeye back. They had called Heather a number of times to see how she was doing, not once did Karl ask how the store was doing because he knew that Heather would be very responsible and take great care. And Heather was doing just that.

It was now 12:30 p.m. on Sunday afternoon, no news, Heather was staying at her parent's home for the week and was hoping to be back on the road late that afternoon to return back to school. Heather did a quick confirmation of the arrival time to see why there was such a delay, she did anticipate her parent's stopping by the shop to do a quick inspection, but not this long of a holdup.

Her search simply added to her concern, the flight had arrived at 8 a.m. with no delays. 'What could be keeping them?' she thought to herself. She tried her father's and mother's cell phones, nothing. She then called the airline to confirm that her parents had been on the flight. To her surprise, Karl and Bonnie had not gotten on the flight.

Her next thought was that they had slept in and missed their flight 'Oh Dad!' she thought to herself.

She called the airline again to see if they had rebooked on another flight, again, NO! Nothing, no notice, no rebook, nothing.

As Heather was sitting and contemplating what to do next, her cell phone rang. It was the French police, letting her know that there had been an accident on the freeway near the airport and that her parents had been killed.

Frozen and overwhelmed in emotion, temporarily she was lost. Amazingly, Heather had managed to composed herself and had took control, and did what had to be done. Karl would have said 'Here goes my little trooper, nobody can stop her when she's on a mission'.

Heather ensured the safe return of her parent's bodies, prepared for the funeral, dealt with the insurance and the lawyers. As devastating as it was, she kept on with the task and also worked at the store, where hundreds of people would dropped in to offer their condolences and to leave flowers. The Mayor dropped by and was surprised to see her there. He offered any assistance she needed, perhaps feeling a little responsible for having sent Karl and Bonnie to Paris. Heather sat with him in the store and talked about how happy her parents were about going. How it had been a dream of her father's and how he had made a wonderful dream come true. She knew not to mention the accident because it would only add to the guilt the Mayor was feeling at the moment, she had him focus on the opportunity he had given them.

A few weeks had gone by when all the family had gotten together to discuss the "Will". Karl and Bonnie had left all four children responsible for the store, and the rest was to be divided equally between all of them.

The grandparents stepped in and said that the store should be put up for sale and money be divided between the kids. Heather was furious and felt betrayed. There was no way that this was in any way acceptable. Their parents dream should live on through them. They should not just give up, their parents had spent so many years working and now that they were gone we should sell. "Not acceptable," she insisted.

Her siblings protested, 'Heather, we need the money' they said.

"Fine" she said angrily, "If it's the money you want, it's the money you will get. What do you estimate the value of the store to be. Tell me!" She was furious.

Her sister quoted a figure, and her brothers agreed.

"Perfect, divide that by four and you will all get that portion from what the house and insurance is valued at. In other words, you will get my share of the 'Money'" she said in a low and serious tone of voice.

Her grandparents were about to say something when Heather spoke again, "Our parents did so much for us, kept a roof over our heads, paid for our education, were always there when needed. Any of you know how hard they worked? Did you know for many years mom had two jobs and dad worked at the store during the day and had a night job? They lived their dream and cared for us, their kids. I believe in family, in security, in something consistent. You all talk about the security of the refinery, well that idea is no longer viable, however, we have a family business that has survived for over 20 years and all you want to do is sell it. You are no better that the corporate people you are screaming at in front of the refinery, you are doing to our parents what strangers are doing to you."

Heather turned to her grandparent's and continued, "And you my dear grandparents, when was the last time you supported your children? I was there when thousands of people were in attendance of a celebration to recognize the hard work and commitment to the community our parents have done. I was there to see that, were you? No! You hide behind the security of big business who have no ties to our family." Heather was not stopping, "If the money is what you want, the money is what you will get, but I will keep my parents alive by keeping the store open. It is the jewel of downtown Boston and my parents built it, so do what you want, you know where I stand." She took the notes she had written down and went to her room.

A few hours later, she was asked to come back down and listen. The siblings had decided that the store should go to the one person who was the most structured and organized, the one person who had the drive to keep the family together, to keep the memory of their parents alive. They would only be silent partners, only to be there if needed, if there was a need at all. The cost was to have the picture of their parents in the store for all to see, for the community of Boston to remember them.

Four years have gone by since that terrible event. Heather is managing the store so successfully that it has increased in size and has designers working in the back on new styles for every season. Heather has been invited and attended the Paris fashion shows for the last five years and has also been recognized as the most distinguished Fashion Boutique in the US and a top contender within the world market.

She had involved her family, including both sets of grandparents in the store growth. All have learned to contribute in one way or another.

Heather understood and put in practice the teachings of her parents. Everyone was different, everyone was special, to respect their time and opinion, but most importantly, to individualize the approach to each person.

"No matter who you are, you can adjust yourself to understand your customer, all you need is to trust yourself, listen and change, it works." Signed Heather ☺

The Blue Buy In

Freddy is a pretty affable fellow who enjoys his life and loves to help others. As a matter of fact he is a volunteer counsellor for troubled young people at the local help centre when he's not working at his regular job as an office manager at the local call centre. He's responsible for the day-to-day maintenance of a fairly large staff of very diverse individuals from all kinds of backgrounds both educationally and culturally and, it's his job to keep things harmonious. The thing is, Freddy had to adjust his radar screen around the age of 45 because he was downsized from the local paper mill which was one of the town's major employers but the move to managing the call centre staff was a good fit as it allowed him to use his nurturing and communication skills. One of Freddy's buddies on the baseball team had suggested he look into the position, the job was available and Freddy jumped at the chance.

Once Freddy settled himself at the call centre he started to occupy himself with learning about not only his new business but his staff. He had many, many challenges to face up to, a good variety of personalities that had created a dysfunctional environment.

In his learning's he met some of the key players in the organization. First Elaine, divorced and mad as hell about her situation but had a voice that would calm the most irated customer down in seconds. Marty, he was one of the accountants at the plant and soon to be retired, not of his choosing. So he was little bitter about the companies mandatory retirement policy. Mary is there as part of a community integration program for the physically challenged and she requires some assistance getting in and out of the building but she loves her job and the chance to interact with other people on the phone. Jonelle is a mother of three with a husband who still works at the mill but he's a problem gambler and its made life for their family very chaotic to say the least. Marilyn is a full time teacher at the local high school who works at the call centre to make extra money to pay for her trips abroad to study art and architecture. Her two true passions. Sherry was one of the front shop merchandisers at the local drug store until the plant closed and the business dropped off. She misses her customers but likes the interaction that she gets with her customers on the phone and it keeps her active although she knows that she could have retired years ago. Jerry works at the mill still but his wife was just diagnosed with a severe illness and will take months to recover and they have two kids in university hundreds of miles away. So the extra money is a big help with their budget.

So you can see that Freddy has quite a group of diverse people to manage and he takes his somewhat parental role very seriously. He's attended management seminars and leadership classes and read every book that he could get his hands on about how to handle crisis and promote harmony in the workplace.

For the most part, Freddy runs a pretty tight ship since taking his role and he and his team have won awards for productivity and excellence in customer service which are very proudly displayed in the outside office for all to see. If you have not guessed it, Freddy is a BLUE.

One day, as luck would have it, Jonelle came bounding in with news of the latest "get rich quick" scheme that she was going to try. In months previous Freddy had made mention that this type of thing was not a good idea in the workplace as people felt pressured to buy and in many cases there had been some justifiably injured feelings which in close quarters didn't bode well. Money was tight in their little community and everyone felt it. So Freddy spoke every day about respect for each other and living up to your true potential. Freddy had worked so hard to make his call centre a model for other call centres in the company. He had arranged for Marty to pick up Mary in the morning to teach him that his situation was not a hard luck as he was always prone to thinking. Marilyn had volunteered to tutor Jonelle's children free of charge when they needed extra help. Sherry got the drugstore to deliver prescriptions to Jerry's home free of charge and they had held a fundraiser for her in the store.

Freddy had a lot to be proud of and understood that the role of a good manager was to create a harmonious workplace where his staff could flourish. When Jonelle came in with the kit and the order forms and the items for sale Freddy took her aside and asked her what she had in mind reminding her gently that perhaps now was not the time or place to set up her pop-up shop.

Jonelle told him that everyone in the office was going to make 'all kinds of money' and that many, many others had made 'millions' with these products and all they had to do was work 'under me' and the person who had signed her up drove an expensive car that the company had just given her for her great sales. "I just know that you will want these products Freddy." Said Jonelle. "They are expensive because they are the best in the world and I am the only one around authorized to sell them. You have to let me do a demonstration for the people in the office Freddy!" pleaded Jonelle. "My bills are not getting paid with my situation being what it is!" "Jonelle," Freddy said patiently, "we have a policy in place here about this kind of thing and you know what everyone is going through at the moment in town."

"Well, if they would just do this like me and sell to everyone they know they would not have to work here in the office at all!" retorted Jonelle defiantly. Freddy looked at her and quietly breathed in. "Jonelle, I am not sure that this is the best way for you to make extra money. I can give you some extra shifts next week as Marilyn is going away for the summer and that should help out and you can have all of Jerry's this week as he is taking his wife away for tests. Would that be helpful?" "Not if I am going to get that car! I want that car and I don't want to really work here for the rest of my life!" declared Jonelle "You're not being fair!" Freddy looked at her with a very puzzled expression and asked her what she could possibly have meant by her last statement to which Jonelle replied "You helped with that fundraiser at the drugstore for Jerry so you should help me too!!" "But that was to help Jerry pay bills Jonelle." Freddy said patiently but to no avail. "I have bills too!!" was the reply from a now reddening Jonelle. "Just look around you Freddy! Is this all you want from your life?!"

Beaten down, Freddy grudgingly gave in. "OK," he said with a sigh, "You can have the lunchroom from 12 to 1. That's your lunch hour but don't take it past that. We are going to have a busy afternoon with the new specials for our customers and I need you at your desk to handle them. They are our business and our wages and this is the last day of the quarter"

"Fine," Jonelle said indignantly and went to her desk. Lunch hour came about and Jonelle had her set-up going full force telling her co-workers how great each new item that came out of the box was and how it would transform their lives. One of the items was a particular tea that was supposed to have miraculous slimming qualities and was needed by the whole team at the call centre as they, according to Jonelle all needed to lose weight now. Jerry, Marilyn, Sherry, Elaine and Mary all were convinced to try and buy the miracle tea and Jonelle made her sales.

Two hours later the phones started to ring off their hooks but the tea was starting to take its effect. Looks of surprise turned to urgent races to bathrooms as the slimming began in earnest. "Get out of the way!" yelled Jerry to Marilyn as they both raced for the restroom. Sherry was in a panic and Mary was in a dire state. "What have you done to us?!" they yelled.

Freddy looked out of his office door and saw the beginnings of chaos taking place. Ring, ring, ring, ring, ring!!! The phones were not being answered and they would not make the quarter for the first time since Freddy had taken over. They would not make their bonus!

Freddy shut his door. There was nothing that could be done. Nothing at all and it was best to stay out of the way until this was done. As mad as he was at the loss of the bonus money Freddy could not help but chuckle at the preposterous scene that was taking place outside his office door and he resolved to teach Jonelle a subtle lesson.

The next day when the haggard looking crew came in the office they found a small sign on Jonelle's partition wall. Nothing blatant, just a small sign that read "**<u>You may have made the sale but you lost your customers</u>**."

CHAPTER 11

CONCLUSION

O ur book was created to add clarity, guidance and care for all of your customers, and to teach you how to reach out to them in the most meaningful way. Each and every day is given to us to discover, to learn and appreciate the people in our lives. Ask yourself, how often do you take the person next to you for granted? How often have you missed wonderful opportunities to meet someone who could have given you a little gift of insight, perspective and awareness of themselves, which in turn would have put your future in a catapult of growth? We ask ourselves, "Why didn't I just say Hello. Or Hi! My name is.....!" That moment could have changed your life forever. Personal fear, for any reason is ultimately your own personal roadblock to growth or moving forward or making that one big sale.

We can never be sure what that next customer walking through that door will bring. What brilliant gift will they deliver in our life unless we are open to receiving it. The concept of understanding people through colours is a simple one that has been around for decades and the most fascinating aspect of it is the simplicity in understanding and applying it.

Understanding one's self is the key to personal success. To know how you will act and react to situations is the answer to who you are. We have been on this wonderful journey and keep traveling the road of adventure each and every day. Your road to discovery was and is not an easy one by any means, however it can be a 'FUN' one. Take a serious look at your history and ask the questions 'Why?' and 'What could have been different?'. These questions have been our motivation for this book and we want to share with the world our findings.

Our personal results have been amazing, our personal relationships have grown and most important our friendship is one that will last forever. All due to the simplicity of understanding each other.

This is our gift to you. We open our doors and welcome you all to join us in working together to create a colourful world of understanding and vibrant discussions. Picture yourself sitting with the person you feel you understand the least and then having a dialogue that will provide you insight in whatever challenge you may be facing. By simply listening and realizing that their picture of the world is very different than yours and that your perspective may not be the best suited to the challenge they are currently facing you are opening up a world of possible solutions.

Being a high **ORANGE and GOLD**, I (**Guy**) lives in a world of personal controversy. Picture a world where you want to be free and spontaneous and next, stop wanting to have fun and all at the same time feeling the need for structure. I want to hold people responsible and maintain a good sense of security. You can quickly see how confusing my life was until I was personally able to see who I truly was and why I thought and acted in a specific fashion. Now I know why I felt know-one understood me. Understanding myself provided me with guidance. You can say that it was like I had found my personal compass to guide me through self-discovery. Finally I stopped the damaging thoughts that were going through my head. I stopped believing the messages given to me from those who did not appreciate who I was and what I had to give.

You see, the journey I have been through is a great one. Discovering myself and the people around me and what they can offer and what I can offer them has never been so much fun. It is now a world of sharing, understanding and collaboration with everyone, it is possible and real. No more will I fear to move forward based on what others may or may not say. My personal approach to people and situations is now one that I enjoy.

My (**Doug's**) story begins around the age of 13 when I was told by a supply teacher in front of my classmates that I had "A great need to be noticed". That statement stung me like hornet for years. All I was doing was being myself. I liked to laugh and joke with my classmates and I liked to be liked. I could not understand why that was so awful but I did not realize that the person talking to me at the time was GOLD driven and I was a BLUE-ORANGE!!! Talk about a square peg in a round hole!!! I felt like that all my life until I started doing the work to make me feel more whole. Finding out who I was then and who I am now has been one of the most liberating things that I have ever experienced. I no longer feel that I need to fit in. I am in. I understand my world from a completely different perspective and it's a lot more pleasant than the one I lived in before. By the way, that comment she made about a need to be noticed was true. I'm a **BLUE-ORANGE** and that's me and its ok.

The straightforwardness and simplicity of this book will provide consistent and positive results, creating effectiveness in your dealings with your customers. We can reach whatever goals we desire if we are armed with confidence and knowledge to bring us there. No need to sit behind the counters and fear that a client may reject your approach. You will be able to observe your client and have the ability to determine what approach would be best suited for them.

Open the doors to a colourful future! See it as bright and joyful as it was meant to be! Create a long-lasting positive impression on your clients and most of all, enjoy the adventure!

Have a colourful journey!!!

Guy & Doug

BIBLIOGRAPHY

Jung, C.G. (1976) Psychological Types - The Collected Works of C.G. Jun, Vol. 6. Princeton, NJ: Princeton University Press.

Keirsey, David & Bates, Marilyn. (1984) Please Understand Me. De. Mar, California: Prometheys Nemesis Book Company

Myers, I.B. (1980) Gifts Differing - Understanding Personality Types. Palo Alto, California: Davies-Black.

Miscisin, M. (2005) Showing Our True Colors. Santa Ana, California: True Colors Inc. Publishing

Made in the USA
Charleston, SC
09 October 2015